Beyond Belief

A Holocaust Survivor's Story

Toby

Hanoch Teller
Based on the testimony of Salek Orenstein

BEYOND BELIEF

A HOLOCAUST SURVIVOR'S STORY

The Toby Press

Beyond Belief: A Holocaust Survivor's Story

First edition, 2025

The Toby Press LLC
POB 8531, New Milford, CT 06776-8531, USA
& POB 4044, Jerusalem 9104001, Israel
www.korenpub.com

Cover photographs and photographs on pages 113–15
courtesy of the Orenstein Family

The publication of this book was made possible through the generous
support of The Jewish Book Trust.

ISBN 978-1-59264-679-1, *paperback*

Printed and bound in the United States

This book is dedicated to those who were murdered at the hands of the Nazis.

ה' יקום דמם

Hershel (Herszek) Tzvi Alter Orenstein (Orensztajn)
January 10, 1896–ca. October 1942 transported to Treblinka extermination camp, father of Salek

Nacha Ella Orenstein (Orensztajn)
1896–ca. October 1942 transported to Treblinka extermination camp, mother of Salek

Yehuda Fischel Orenstein (Orensztajn)
1922–1945, murdered in Schlieben concentration camp, brother of Salek

Schifra Leah Orenstein (Orensztajn)
1928–ca. October 1942 transported to Treblinka extermination camp, sister of Salek

Salek Orenstein's parents-in-law:

Shmuel Merel
October 11, 1890–August 28, 1942, murdered in Auschwitz, father-in-law of Salek

Mindel Merel
January 8, 1890–May 18, 1941, murdered in Rivsaltes concentration camp, mother-in-law of Salek

In 1996, Salek Orenstein presented each of his children with a book compiled by Martin Gilbert, called The Boys. *It is the story of 732 young concentration camp survivors, children who shared wartime experiences that were terrible beyond imagination. Some of his personal experiences are recorded in that book. Salek's dedication to his children reads as follows:*

To my dear children,
May these horrific personal memories and testimonies of the very few Jewish survivors be an eternal documented lesson to all the future generations – to stand on guard against the antisemitic world who never relinquished its aim and wish to destroy us.
Love Dad, Saba, 4th November 1996

&

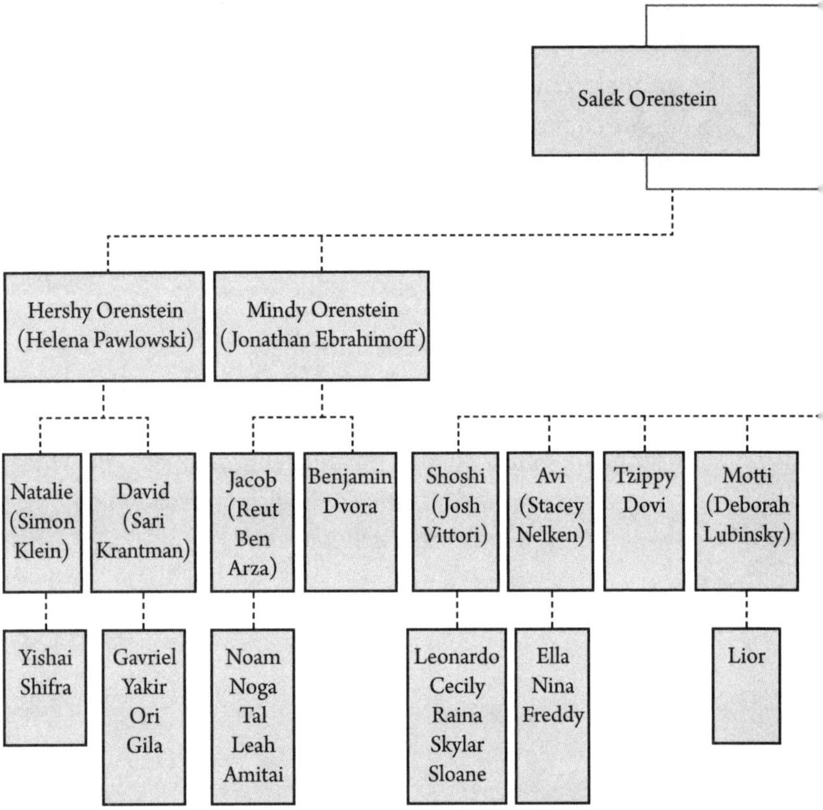
Salek Orenstein
Hershy Orenstein (Helena Pawlowski)
Mindy Orenstein (Jonathan Ebrahimoff)
Natalie (Simon Klein)
David (Sari Krantman)
Jacob (Reut Ben Arza)
Benjamin Dvora
Shoshi (Josh Vittori)
Avi (Stacey Nelken)
Tzippy Dovi
Motti (Deborah Lubinsky)
Yishai Shifra
Gavriel Yakir Ori Gila
Noam Noga Tal Leah Amitai
Leonardo Cecily Raina Skylar Sloane
Ella Nina Freddy
Lior

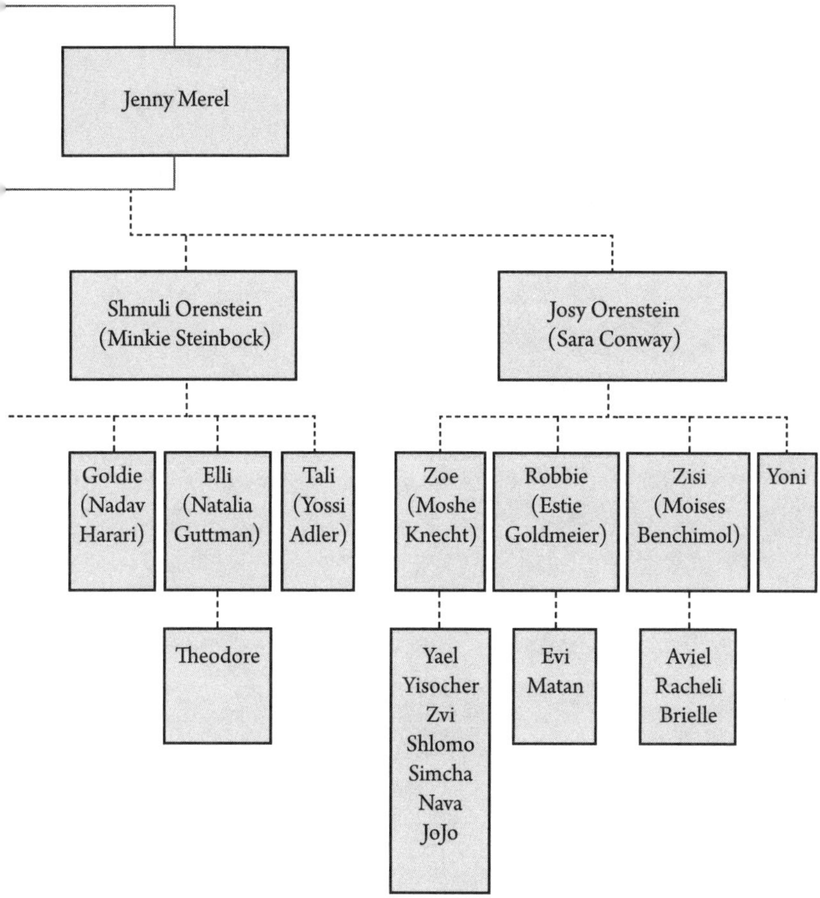
Jenny Merel
Shmuli Orenstein
(Minkie Steinbock)
Josy Orenstein
(Sara Conway)
Goldie
(Nadav
Harari)
Elli
(Natalia
Guttman)
Tali
(Yossi
Adler)
Zoe
(Moshe
Knecht)
Robbie
(Estie
Goldmeier)
Zisi
(Moises
Benchimol)
Yoni
Theodore
Yael
Yisocher
Zvi
Shlomo
Simcha
Nava
JoJo
Evi
Matan
Aviel
Racheli
Brielle

Contents

Preface xiii

Acknowledgments xvii

Introduction by Hanoch Teller xix

1. Life in the *Shtetl* 1

2. The Quiet Before the Storm 9

3. Lifecycle Events and the Greatest *Simcha* 18

4. First Shadows 26

5. Liquidation of the Jewish Community in Opatow 33

6. Road to Hell on Earth 39

7. A Very Narrow Escape from Death 48

8. Chance Meeting: My Yellow Brother! 57

9. Tortured Beyond Human Endurance 64

10. Buchenwald Concentration Camp 70

11. Spring 1945 – Allied Bombers 75

12. The Death Train 80

13. A Flicker of Hope 88

14. The Beginning of a Long Recuperation 95

15. It Was Love at First Sight (Yes, First Sight!) 100

Postscript 103

Afterword 105

Eulogy for My Father 109

Glossary 117

Preface

When it comes to loss, people speak of time as the great healer. I can tell you; time is not a great healer. Sometimes it does not heal at all, for it puts an ever-expanding distance between the living and the dead. With death, an axis of love is broken. A world within a world breaks its moorings, never to return.

It began with the Holocaust, when time stopped. A horrible crime, visited by the wicked on the innocent. The Holocaust was not only sinister and horrifying, but also an event not easy to comprehend in conventional terms. It was an event that has been written down in its own code, a code which had to be broken first to make understanding possible.

From a philosophical standpoint, my father's suffering and the years since his passing have taught me the hidden potentials revealed in his personal account. His unique encounters and rare combination of circumstances describe the Holocaust while he undertook the unrewarding and painful task of recounting events that we (and he) preferred to leave unspoken. Victimization of Jews and the progressively dehumanizing impact of coercive authority reign. Not enough has been done after the Holocaust to disarm these conceivably gruesome effects. Over seventy years later, the terrible relics that concentration camps hold are disintegrating, and with the passing of its last witnesses, we are now faced with unprecedented questions about how to preserve the memory of the Holocaust.

This book is intended as a small and modest contribution to what seems to be the long-overdue task of bringing one survivor's story to bear witness. Through the eyes of a child driven by grief and horror, it is testimonial proof of the events it embodies. Journeys of brutalizing squalor; trains leading directly to gas chambers; kilos of human hair shorn from the living and from corpses; barracks; barbed-wire fencing; watchtowers; starvation; indescribable human suffering; violence; cruelty; dying and death... an abundance of evidence.

My father's account not only passes on his legacy to future generations, but it is a means of keeping his memory alive. It is a way of acknowledging the grandparents who gave me life but whom I never had the privilege of knowing. They never had longevity (אריכות ימים), for the Nazis systematically persecuted and destroyed them all. If there were adequate words rather than just ashes, perhaps the pain would be less. Something to hold on to. The heart demands it. But life goes on. It can be no other way, of course.

This foreword would not be complete without acknowledging two of my father's friends who also survived forced labor camps and death marches. Even as a little girl I knew who they were. They had accents, and like us, they had few relatives. My father, Sender Riseman, and Solly Irving were members of the group of 732 young concentration camp survivors who became known as "The Boys." Proud of their Jewish identity, they rebuilt their lives in London and became lifelong friends. These "boys" deserve a special mention for their unerring belief in all things Jewish, and in the State of Israel. Solly would engage young audiences, who would listen in silence to his personal experiences of war, abandonment, imprisonment, and survival. In their lifetime, my father Salek Orenstein and his two friends became a living bridge between destruction and rebirth. Our families established friendships across three generations and till today share Shabbat meals together.

My father's story bears witness to the triumphs of the human spirit. It is the story of a man who was proud of his heritage and faith. It is the story of a Jew and a Zionist who pledged continued moral commitment to remain faithful to God's covenant, which he might so easily have rejected. This story is his gift to the next generations and reminds us that it is up to us to ensure, "Never Again."

Mindy Ebrahimoff (née Orenstein)

Acknowledgments

We would like to thank Judy Goodkin for helping us create this book. With patience, time, and creativity she encouraged our father to find his voice and transcribed his oral testimony into writing. This took skill, sensitivity, and compassion, and we are extremely grateful for her hard work and dedication. Her manuscript forms the essence of this book, without which its publication would not have been possible.

We would also like to thank Koren Publishers, Matthew Miller, Aryeh Grossman, Reuven Ziegler, Caryn Meltz, Debbie Ismailoff, Gila Chitiz, and Tomi Mager, who made distinctive and often invaluable contributions to this book.

Finally, a sincere thank you to Rabbi Hanoch Teller for writing *Beyond Belief.*

Family Orenstein

Introduction

For urban dwellers, life in a town is nearly unfathomable (albeit, perhaps quaint). Reducing even further to townlet, village, and hamlet, somewhere along the way would be the *shtetl,* the Yiddish diminutive for *shtot,* which means "town."

Figuratively, the word "*shtetl*" implies a small community (although it need not have been one) in Eastern Europe prior to World War II. It equally implies a simple life, greatly governed by religion or at least tradition, where a Jew, usually much of the population – despite privation and arduous labor – always felt at home.

The twin pillars of the *shtetl* were *Yiddishkeit* (Jewish governance of all aspects of life) and *menshlichkeit* (moral sensitivity and noble behavior toward one's fellow man). No two ideals could have enjoyed a more symbiotic relationship than was practiced in the *shtetl,* where the sacred and the profane were seamlessly fused. The *shtetl's* grounding in *Yiddishkeit* and *mentschlichkeit* were most readily discerned in the synagogue, the home, and the market.

For most Western Jews, exposure to the *shtetl* came from the 1964 Broadway musical *Fiddler on the Roof.* Based on the stories of

Sholom Aleichem, and set in the Pale of Settlement in 1905, the plot concerns how Tevye, the *shtetl* milkman and father of five daughters, endeavors to maintain his religious fidelity as outside influences and the czar's edicts undermine the traditions of his family.

When *Fiddler* debuted on Broadway in the 1960s the majority of American Jewry had little connection to a *shtetl,* nostalgic or otherwise. On the contrary, American Jews, by and large, certainly those who could afford to, were moving away from religious centers that were once immigrant neighborhoods. Suddenly, Tevye was their first lesson in Tradition.

And whereas *Fiddler on the Roof* conveys how tightly knit the Jewish communities were, it fails to portray how paramount Torah study and boundless acts of kindness were in the *shtetl.* And this brings us to *Beyond Belief,* the most intimate, informative, and enchanting description of a non-fiction *shtetl* I have ever read or heard about.

In *Beyond Belief,* Salek Orenstein recounts in rich detail what he witnessed growing up in the *shtetl* of Apt (Opatow), providing the readers with a personal, up-front view of a world that was, from the water shlepper to the rebbetzin, from the grain merchant to the beggars, to the *Shabbos goy,* and absolutely everyone in between with humor, pathos, and angst.

It should be noted, as Salek makes clear, that Apt is not just any *shtetl.* It was the home of four of the major founders of the early hasidic movement, a fact that transformed this *klaynshtetl* into a megalopolis – by shtetl standards – of over sixty-six hundred souls by the time Salek frolicked on its dirt paths.

When Reb Yisrael of Koznitz (Kozieice), an early leader of the hasidic movement, was born in Apt in 1733 there were less than one thousand Jews living in the entire vicinity. In the late eighteenth century Reb Moshe Leib of Sasow, one of the most revered names of early *Hasidus,* established his court in Apt, rendering it a major hasidic center. Reb Yaakov Yitzchak of Przysucha, renowned as the *Yid HaKodesh*, also graced Apt with his presence, causing the population to swell to three times its size.

And then Reb Avraham Yehoshua Heschel, the saintly rebbe who had led various communities beforehand, settled in Apt. Reb Avraham Yehoshua was so enchanted with Apt that he requested that his name always be associated with the town, and indeed he is eponymously known as the Apta Rav (Rabbi of Apt).

The Rebbe of Apt also merited another moniker, which his contemporaries – all disciples of the famous Reb Elimelech of Lizhensk – and his disciples attested that he richly deserved. The Rebbe of Apt was known and revered far and wide as the *Ohev Yisrael*, a sobriquet adopted from his magnum opus.

Reb Elimelech of Lizhensk said about his prized disciple, "His name is reflective of his very being. He has *ahavas Yisrael* (love for his fellow Jew) like Avraham Avinu, and a princely look like Yehoshua; his mind is as sharp as his grandfather Reb Heschel." Reb Elimelech once commented to the Chozeh of Lublin, "The very prayers of the Apta Rav build the celestial Temple and insert within them the ark and the tablets."

The Apta Rav was the youngest of Reb Elimelech's primary disciples, which made him the oldest of the torchbearers of the hasidic flame for the next generation. His word was a command to anyone with hasidic allegiance in Poland.

Of this fabled and holy shtetl of Apt less than three hundred survived the Nazi onslaught. Salek Orenstein was one of the few survivors, and through his enchanting and at times heartbreakingly stark memoir, the reader is able to vicariously experience *shtetl* life and the gruesome closing of this glorious chapter of Jewish history.

Hanoch Teller

Chapter One

Life in the *Shtetl*

Salek Orenstein was born and raised in the Polish town of Opatow, better known to the Jewish world as "Apt." Many have heard of this tiny town – it took only ten minutes to traverse – because of her proudest son, Rabbi Yehoshua Heschel, better known as the *Ohev Yisrael*, the disciple of Reb Elimelech of Lizhensk.

Apt was an economically depressed town, though rich in Torah scholarship. There was never a shortage of *rabbanim* in Apt to rule on halachic issues and they were consulted all the time.

The heart of Apt's economy was the "market" that was conducted every Wednesday. On this day people would come from the countryside to sell their wares, including ducks, cows, and all sorts of livestock and agricultural products. At the market they would also take the opportunity to purchase any dry goods they needed for the week.

Most people in the *shtetl* were involved in small-scale trading. They worked as tailors, shoemakers, store owners, and the like. Salek's father, Hershel, was a timber and wheat merchant who was in business with three of his cousins.

Salek saw his father only on Shabbos; during the week the head of the family was away on business. Each day, which started early in the morning, was devoted to traveling across the countryside to meet with Polish landlords on their estates. It was there that Salek's father made his purchases of wheat and timber. Before World War II he also did a fair amount of trade with Germany.

Salek's mother, Nacha Ella, was a housewife who was assisted by a non-Jewish woman named Zosia. Even though she spoke an excellent Yiddish (she was brought up in the Orenstein home) Zosia was never relied upon to help with the cooking.

A moderate upheaval took place in the Orenstein home twice a month when an elderly, non-Jewish woman would arrive to do the laundry. Like any fairly large family, they generated a good amount of laundry, but they did not have the machinery to deal with it.

The laundry lady would haul in her own zinc tub and place it on the stove to boil. Then the soiled clothes would be placed within it to soak. This method was no different from how the Orensteins dealt with their dirty dishes except that the laundry lady had some cleaning agents to add to the water.

After the clothes had been laundered, they would be taken up to the loft and hung out to dry. The laundry lady would return only a few days later to take down the load before placing it through a mangle as a prelude to ironing. All in all, it was a major operation.

As the youngest boy, Salek did a lot of chores around the house. His older siblings were far more adept at getting out of most jobs. His little sister, Shifra Leah, was considered too small for this kind of work. Nacha Ella made sure, though, that Salek was rewarded for his efforts.

Sour milk, butter, and other items that needed to be kept cool were stored in the cellar. Salek was assigned to transport items to and from the cellar, and he would go down there with the aid of a candle.

Salek was also entrusted with taking the chickens to the *shochet*. After slaughtering the animals and extracting the blood, the *shochet* would place the chickens back into the basket in such a way that by the time Salek returned home there were no longer any visible traces of blood.

After the chicken that Salek brought home had been plucked and cleaned by the non-Jewish maid, his mother would open up the bird herself in order to inspect its insides and *kasher* it with salt. Occasionally she would discover some imperfections, such as a liver that had a strange appearance or a fracture in a small bone, which might render the chicken non-kosher. Naturally Salek was dispatched to the *Rav* to verify the fowl's *kashrus*.

Salek arrived at the rabbi's house and was greeted by the rebbetzin who would inquire regarding the nature of the visit. She would then go to summon the rabbi. The rabbi would place the chicken on the table and open it up. The first question he would ask was, "Is this for Shabbos?" Salek assumed that his response had some bearing on the ruling.

Presumably, if the fowl was intended for the Shabbos meal and there wasn't enough time to find a replacement, the rabbi would attempt to be more lenient in his *pesak* – but not before launching an investigation. "Was this bone broken before or after *kashering*?" Salek would shrug his shoulders in ignorance. If the imperfection was borderline, generally speaking, the *rav* would approve it and instruct him, "Tell the Mammeh it is kosher."

The boy's other weekly chores included bringing the *cholent* to the baker on Friday afternoon. The Orensteins' pot had a special blue and red ribbon tied around it for the purpose of identification. This way when Salek collected the steaming *cholent* on Shabbos morning he was able to recognize the Orenstein pot immediately and not bring home somebody else's food!

Beggars were a regular fixture at the Orenstein home, except on Shabbos. Otherwise, from the early morning until late at night the needy would camp out in the Orenstein apartment, usually without bothering to knock before entering. The majority of the beggars were women, who wore shawls over their heads and often carried babies, which was most effective in ensuring a sympathetic response.

When Salek was old enough, he was placed in charge of the vital task of providing for the needy visitors. Basically, all he had to do was distribute the bread that his mother had already baked and sliced.

Sometimes the hungry would complain that they did not want bread for they had already had enough that day. What they wanted, they insisted, was a few lumps of sugar. Once they caught sight of the kettle simmering on the stove their visits would always become more protracted. They would hold their hands over it to warm themselves and invariably ask to sip some hot water.

Like virtually every other dwelling in Apt, the Orenstein home did not have running water. Some residents had a pump, but usually the water for daily needs was stored in a big barrel in the kitchen.

Jewish water carriers would refill this barrel once or twice a day. The water carriers would take advantage of their services by asking Mrs. Orenstein to serve them a little hot water (with a dash of tea) if they saw the kettle standing on the stove. "*Gib mir a bissale heiss wasser*. Give me a bit of hot water," they would beg.

Zisskind was one of Apt's water carriers and Salek would provide him with a cup of hot water – but it came with a price. "Zisskind!" the little boy would demand. "*Tehillim perek heh, pasuk lamed-alef*? *Pesachim, perek chamishi, der dritten Mishnah*!" No matter what he was asked, this humble water carrier knew the answer without a moment's hesitation. He knew the entire Bible and Talmud by heart!

One day, Zisskind somberly informed Salek, "Your water barrel is lined with dirt."

As there was no filtration system, the water from the well was polluted with fine deposits that gradually settled at the bottom.

Zisskind refused to fill the barrel until it had been thoroughly cleaned. Alas, this *talmid chacham*'s agenda was not merely to ensure the purity of the water...

"If you give me a *gleizalle tei,* I will take the barrel downstairs, wash it out, and you will have nice, pure water."

Salek must have been seven or eight years old at the time, but he was wise enough to realize that clean water was better than dirty water, and the two of them made a deal.

When Zisskind saw the little boy huffing and puffing to ignite the flame for the hot water, he suggested adding a bit of paraffin. In his eagerness, Zisskind spilled the paraffin, resulting in a singed beard. Eventually he got his drink and Salek never mentioned the episode to his mother.

Cooking in the *shtetl* was arduous. Every time the stove needed to be lit it was necessary to climb into the loft and haul down timber and coal. Then began the hard part: It was a Herculean task to light the stove. The wood was often too moist for kindling, so paper and other ignitable materials were added to move things along. And all the while a crew would simultaneously puff their lungs out so that the spark would catch.

That's why hot water was such a coveted prize and Zisskind had to bargain so much. When he would depart with his empty pails his lips were aflame, reciting *Tehillim* or folios of Talmud by heart. No matter where he went and no matter what time of day, he was always engaged in his devotions. Despite an obviously rough life punctuated by abject poverty, Zisskind would always boom, "*Baruch Hashem*!" when asked how he was doing.

Feivel the milkman was another fixture in Apt. Everyone knew when old Feivel was coming to make his deliveries. He would trudge from house to house every morning – no matter the weather – hauling two large buckets of milk with a zinc measuring cup attached by a chain to one of the buckets. The cup would rattle and thump as Feivel shuffled around town making his deliveries.

The other way that you knew he was coming was his unmistakable visage. Feivel was a small man with broad shoulders and a long, wide, red beard which practically covered his entire face. When he spoke, you saw the beard moving up and down and you could hear a voice, but you could never quite see through the crimson forest to pinpoint where his mouth was.

Feivel's attire consisted of a sackcloth apron tied around his belly with a red hand towel of sorts oddly attached. This cloth was versatile; it was used to wipe Feivel's beard and it also had two knots within it which functioned as a bank. One knot housed the coins that he used to provide change for his paying customers, and the other knot was allocated for coins that he would save for his personal Shabbos purchases.

Whenever Feivel was running late with his deliveries he would declare: "I first went to the ladies who have just given birth," and base his tardiness on an elusive text. "*Azoi shteit geshriben!* Is this not what it says?" As members of a kindly, sharing community, the residents of Apt understood that Feivel was loosely ascribing his actions to a Torah precept that mandated looking after the needy first. Had there actually been as many new births as Feivel claimed, then tiny Apt would have been triple Lodz's population!

In Apt, as in so many other *shtetlach,* one Jew was always ready to extend himself on behalf of his brethren. The sense of kindred and brotherhood was heightened by the fact that the residents were surrounded by illiterate and hostile non-Jews. Apt's Catholics received their basic education from the local priests, who exhorted the masses to hate the Jews, who killed their god. If the non-Jews had not required employment by the Jews they never would have tolerated or spared the Jewish majority.

***

Salek's father's three cousins were his business partners in the grain business, just as their fathers had been. The goods were transported to the nearest station by horse and coach in the summer and by sleigh in the winter.

Except for an occasional taxi that was traveling from point A to point B with Apt in the middle, motorized vehicles never ventured into the *shtetl.* The nearest railway station was over twelve miles away in Ostrowiec, and any major journey had to begin there.

Salek's father conducted his business slightly outside the town boundary, just beyond the arched gateway to Opatow that, with the Church wall, formed the official entrance to the town. He had a large yard, a stable with four horses, and a barn. A family of storks nested on the roof of the barn every spring. When the youngsters of Opatow saw the storks flying overhead, they always knew that summer was approaching and they would joke, "The storks are bringing the babies!" Salek enjoyed watching the mother stork feeding her chicks on the top of their barn, their beaks open wide. It was a very special sight.

Salek visited Ostrowiec only once. This visit was long in coming, for Hershel had never agreed to take Salek along to Ostrowiec, until one day he finally caved in. That was the first and only time that Salek ever met his older cousin Avraham, who was a left-wing Zionist, and the only family member who did not have a beard.

Avraham was a very handsome man; his wife was rather stout with a pronounced squint. Everyone assumed that Hershel's cousin must have married for money, for why else would he have consented to marry someone with such an obvious deformity? Their daughter, however, was adorable, with a head full of blond curls.

The first time that Salek ever saw a train was during this visit to Ostrowiec. It was also the first time that he had ever seen a real city. The Jewish population in the city was more than three times that of Apt, which is why Ostrowiec had a world-famous rabbi.

Salek never wanted to leave cosmopolitan Ostrowiec, but at the end of the day he was ordered into his father's horse and buggy. He spent the drive home pestering his father about the locomotive, asking about its steam and wondering how such a giant machine could move without horses. When Salek returned to Apt he told all of his friends about what he had seen, and since no one else had ever seen a train before, he was able to wildly exaggerate and spin magic with his tale.

As primitive a mode of transportation as the sleigh may seem, in the eyes of the youngsters it was very appealing. When Salek would ride in the coach, holding the reins and guiding the two horses harnessed with sleigh bells all by himself, he was sure that his heart would burst from pride.

***

Salek's father had a large yard, a stable with four horses, a storehouse, and a barn, all located outside the town boundary. Since grain kept in sacks for a long period will ferment, they would lay out the grain thinly and regularly rake it to aerate the grain and avoid having moisture build up.

The father of Zosia the maid fed and watered the horses, and at times he also acted as coachman, accompanying Salek's father on business trips in the winter. This enabled Salek's father to sit wrapped up in his great coat to keep warm and avoid hypothermia.

Salek's greatest enjoyment was to accompany his father on his road trips to the wealthy landlords who resided in the countryside. It was a treat to watch the farmers plowing their land or harvesting their crops and significantly more appreciated than spending the day in school.

Chapter Two

The Quiet Before the Storm

Education in the *shtetl* began at a young age. Salek was enrolled in *cheder* from the age of two, when he, like all of the other toddlers, would be brought to school by the *belfer,* a Pied Piper type of figure who collected the young boys from their homes. He used to shout, "I'll come and fetch you at nine o'clock!" which was a ridiculous assertion because he didn't have a watch and could only approximate the time.

The children in *cheder* sat on a little bench about twelve inches off the floor, directly before a chalkboard adorned with the *Alef-Beis*. The *melamed* in Apt was a toothless, comical character. It was rather hard to take him seriously because every time he opened his mouth to teach, he sounded like a small bird gasping for air. Regardless, he got the job done and by the age of five the boys were well versed in *Chumash* and Rashi.

Salek loved most aspects of *cheder,* but what he loved the most was when his mother gave him pocket money to buy a treat. There wasn't a variety of treats in Apt, but one solitary one was to

Salek's perfect delight.... Outside the *cheder* sat an ancient-looking lady with a face full of wrinkles. Her name was Yentel Beila and her head was wrapped in a coarse covering studded with fake pearls and colored stones.

Yentel Beila sat on a straw-packed cushion, on top an old, brown stool, swathed in heavy cloaks and shawls to keep her warm. In front of her was a stove of sorts heated by glowing charcoals. Over this contraption she roasted a rack of steaming, Polish-variety chestnuts. Her sleeves, her shawl, and even her chin were blackened by the fire which she tended to all day long.

For five grosz Salek was able purchase a handful of these *boobes,* which Yentel Beila wrapped in a newspaper. With the *boobes* in hand, Salek made a royal entrance to the *cheder,* causing the little school boys to beg and plead for a taste, offering anything and everything – at some future, elusive date – in return.

When Salek was eight years old his mother gave him the greatest gift a boy his age could have ever hoped for: a lantern to illuminate his way home from school on dark winter nights. *Nothing* could have made him happier.[1]

The winters throughout that region were very harsh and the streets piled deep in snow. On those early mornings and nights, Salek would light the candle in his lantern and walk proudly through the town with a trail of children following behind his light. The children would implore Salek for the privilege of holding the lantern "for just a minute" or "only three steps."

The lantern was a universal source of envy, not only for the illumination it shed, but also for the modicum of warmth that it provided.

***

1. It did not take long to walk anywhere, as the *cheder*, the *mikve* and the *beis hakevaros* were all concentrated in a few streets.

Some children only attended *cheder*, but from the age of six, Salek went to a secular school in the morning before transferring to *cheder* in the afternoon. There were two schools in Apt aside from the *cheder*: a small Jewish school, established by a Zionist named Weissblum called "Tarbut," and a Catholic school.

Salek went to the non-Jewish school, as did the children from other devout families. They felt that it was preferable for their sons and daughters to be educated in the Catholic school than, *chas vechalila*, learn a distorted version of the Torah that the nonreligious Jewish school would provide.

The torment of the Jewish children in the Catholic school was never-ending. One morning Salek was assaulted by someone in school who shoved pork down his throat for a laugh. The teachers, none of whom were Jewish, never intervened, no matter what the atrocity.

The anguish was not over after school either, as the Jewish students were frequently attacked on their way home. It was commonplace for children to throw stones at them and push them around. There were eleven Jewish children in Salek's class – six girls and five boys. Altogether there were thirty children in Salek's class, and the majority felt duty bound to assault the minority.

Once a week a Jewish teacher would come to the school to provide religious instruction. The rest of the time the Jewish pupils were not allowed to cover their heads and had to join the Catholics in their prayers. The Jewish children were brighter and better achievers than the non-Jewish students, which only served to exacerbate an already very volatile hatred.

When he grew older, Salek began to learn Talmud in *cheder*. Salek's instructor was a young Belzer Hasid named Reb Shloimaleh.[2] He would always teach Talmud standing, wearing his tefillin. From time to time, Reb Shloimaleh would reach up to a

2. Like virtually all of the other Jewish residents of Apt, he was murdered by the Nazis.

high shelf where there was a tall glass with some brown particles floating inside. Using his middle and forefingers he would extract a raisin from the glass without even looking up.

For all Salek could tell, this was the man's nourishment for the entire day. Reb Shloimaleh was rail thin with zero interest in food; he was totally absorbed in Torah learning. He was a good teacher, and thanks to him Salek always had a *vertel* or two to repeat at the Shabbos table, as well as a fluent knowledge of the Gemara.

Salek's father's appearance was rather modern for that period. He wore a short beard, as did his cousins, and he never shaved it. But Salek's grandfather, Avrohom Orenstein, wore a *shtreimel* on Shabbos. Salek would go to see him on Shabbos afternoons, and sit with him and read what he had learned in *Chumash* or Rashi. His grandfather always gave him a sweet for coming and if he did well, he would give him an extra sweet when he left, too. Avrohom always sat with a Gemara or Midrash or *Chumash* open. The *seforim* were timeworn, missing their bindings, and had pages that were ripped, detached, and black from over-use. Seeing his grandfather with an old Gemara, Salek naively asked one day, "Zeide, why don't you get a new one?" Avrohom replied, "I know this Gemara and this Gemara knows me."

Avrohom lived outside the town gate in a single-story building with a wooden roof, partially thatched. He was married twice. His second wife, Sorah, was a widow and had a son Moishe, from her previous marriage. Moishe worked in a Jewish bank and his style of dress was decidedly modern. He wore a hat and a smart jacket – not the traditional, old-fashioned *Yiddishe* cap and *kapoteh*. Sorah came from a family that ran a textile business, and she opened a branch in Opatow at the corner of the marketplace. She sold cloth to the non-Jewish customers from the surrounding villages and the farmers who came to the market each Wednesday. Salek's job was to help her put the bales of material back onto the shelves at the end of the day. His grandfather very rarely came to the shop, and if he did he would sit outside with a *sefer*.

It was Moishe who encouraged Salek to ask his father for music lessons. He remembered that when Salek's aunt got married, the young boy spent the entire wedding gazing up with fascination at the *klezmer* musicians. The *klezmer* bands would play at weddings and whenever there was a *hachnosas Sefer Torah*. They would even play at non-Jewish weddings because the *goyim* did not play musical instruments. Whenever a Polish wedding procession went by, it was the Jewish *klezmer* bands that accompanied them!

Salek followed Moishe's advice and asked his father for violin lessons. They went to see the oldest member of the *klezmer* band, Chazkel, an ancient man with a flowing white beard, to inquire if he would be Salek's tutor. A deal was struck, and Thursday afternoons, Salek went to the musician's small one-room apartment tucked away in an attic. A big double bed dominated the space – although there was no sign of a wife to share it – covered with a heavy red bedspread and thick fringes hanging down. Next to the window was the music stand, always displaying sheets of music. "Chazkel," Salek would often beg, "please play something for me! I am not happy with the music that I play – it's got no *ta'am*, no *reyach*." Chazkel saw immediately that Salek's dissatisfaction stemmed from the fact that he was a small boy trying to play on a full-sized violin. "I'll talk to your father," he promised. "I know someone who has a small violin, just right for you." As promised, a small violin was procured for Salek.

One day Chazkel asked rhetorically, "You want to hear some music?" He pulled some tattered-looking music sheets from a drawer and placed them on the music stand. He then pulled himself up straight – not a simple feat for a man that appeared at least a hundred years old – and performed a piece by Weinarski that was so beautiful that Salek remembered it into his old age. He closed his eyes and was in Heaven, for he had never heard anything so wonderful in his life.

Chazkel's son visited him one day while Salek was having his lesson. He laughed at the two of them and commented, "What do you want to teach him music for? He's got a rich father, so he won't be a *klezmer,* he'll be a businessman!" This fellow knew all about the precarious lifestyle of a musician, because he earned his living wandering through all the tiny villages that dotted the countryside near Opatow, often playing music at non-Jewish weddings and feasts.

Although the amenities in Opatow, like all Polish towns, were quite primitive, it did possess some culture. Even young people could converse about music and philosophy. The only source of information was reading, and the only radio in town was owned by the proprietor of a pub named Zeifman whose clientele was non-Jewish.[3]

Salek's father made his own schnapps using cherries that he had gathered in the country. He washed the cherries, removed the stalks, added sugar and stored the mixture in large bottles on top of a tall cupboard for a month or two until it had acquired some strength. This liqueur he would save for a *lechayim* for a proper occasion like a *zucher* or a *simche*. He was not a casual drinker, but others would buy vodka, which had the added virtue of generating heat.

As far as Salek was concerned, Shabbos began on Thursday when he had to go to both the *shochet* and the baker. It was also then that his mother would go to the marketplace and buy a live carp, which would move into the Orenstein's washing bowl. Salek loved to throw breadcrumbs into the water and watch the fish consume them. It was far more exciting than *cheder,* and whenever he

3. During the war they were not allowed to own radios, but nevertheless, Salek and others would listen to the news from London on Zeifman's radio.

could get away with it he would claim that he was ill on a Thursday so that he could stay home and engage in this thrilling pastime.

In preparation for Shabbos, Salek's mother baked challos. This was a talent that required far more skill than ordinary bread making. Just as the dough began to rise, the process had to be interrupted by additional kneading, followed by braiding the strips of dough into the unique challa shape.

The job of brushing the bread with egg yolk was left to Salek, and he took great pride in the special shine that it produced. Salek would also carry the finished product to the baker, who for remuneration baked them in his oven.

All the baker did was provide the oven, and the Orensteins (and the baker's other customers) were fully responsible for removing the bread at just the right time. If one tarried in removing his own challos he was left with no choice but to purchase the commercial challos that the baker produced.

On Fridays, a short man named Reb Moishe visited the Orensteins with a small bottle of wine which he clandestinely hid within his *kapoteh*. "Why are you hiding it in your coat?" Salek wanted to know.

"I wish to keep it out of sight of the non-Jews." The little boy deduced from this that if the wine was ever exposed to non-Jews, then it would not be fit for *Kiddush*.

Reb Moishe would pull a little cup out of his right pocket, which he used to gauge four measures of raisin wine. He then poured the wine into one of the Orensteins' decanters. Salek watched him intently and would challenge, "You haven't given us a full cup! Your measures aren't accurate."

His critique was based on the fact that Reb Feivel the milkman had a much larger measuring cup.

"You should see Reb Feivel's measuring cup!" the young boy protested. "It is much bigger than yours!"

"*Oy! Red nicht kein narischkeiten!* Ach! Don't prattle such silliness!" Reb Moishe snorted with dismissal. "*Er hot sore milch; ich hob gutten wein*! He sells sour milk, while I provide quality wine!"

How exactly the quality of the product impacted upon a different standard of measurement was beyond young Salek, but he was certain that his protest was not as "silly" as Reb Moishe contended.

In Apt, every single shop was closed on Shabbos. Indeed, by Friday afternoon the main street resembled a ghost town. In the Orenstein home, like in every other Jewish residence, the table was adorned with the family's finest tablecloth, plates, and cutlery. Any attractive item in the house made it onto the table to grace the atmosphere with specialness and sanctity.

The home possessed a unique aroma as the freshly baked challos emitted a heavenly scent that fused with the smell of the sweet wine and the pungent dishes stewing on the stove. The stove was not very large, so Mrs. Orenstein prearranged for a non-Jew to come up and add some wood to the fire so that it would burn for the duration of Shabbos. The non-Jew would be compensated for his or her efforts with a large piece of challa and sometimes was invited to join the family for a glass of tea.

This seemingly paltry remuneration was greatly valued by the local peasants, who dined on poor, tasteless, rough black bread. Challa was a delicacy of the highest order and they cherished a hot drink no less than Zisskind the water carrier.

The apartment was bathed in a romantic glow emanating from the candles, whose number correlated to the number of children. The nest of warmth and tranquility was shared with guests who were either poor strangers passing through town, local indigents or neighbors, or friends joining the Orensteins for Russian tea and abundant cake.

The custom in Apt was that the truly poor would gather in the synagogue Friday evening and wait at the door to be invited for a Shabbos meal. At least one from this group would always come home with the Orenstein family. These people came in all sizes, personality types, and temperaments. Some were clean shaven, others had scraggly beards; some had closely cropped haircuts and others hadn't seen a barber in years; some were as thin as rails and others were so heavy that it took great effort for them to scale the steps leading to the apartment.

Salek liked to reminisce about a man who – so different from the rest – would never plunge directly into his meal, but would wait, courteously, not partaking of a morsel until everyone else had been served. There was no question that he was just as hungry as all of the other guests, but his polite disposition always governed his behavior and endeared him to the Orensteins. Salek's father would usually invite this gentleman to attend the subsequent meal on Shabbos.

There was one occasion when a man came to us with his clothes in tatters. His trousers were so torn that you could literally see his shirt tails sticking out of them. As he sat down at our table, my father looked at him and said "Reb Yid, come with me." They left us eating in the kitchen and went over together to the bedroom. This puzzled me. I wanted to know where my father was going, so I followed him. What I saw next was truly an unforgettable sight. My father was taking off his own trousers and giving them to that poor man. As he stood there, trouserless, he looked across to where I was and said simply, "Ask your mother to come in."

Mrs. Orenstein came in and questioned while removing another pair of trousers from the closet for her husband. "Are you insane? Why did you have to give him your best trousers? They matched your *kapoteh* perfectly!"

Before any of the visitors left the Shabbos table, Mrs. Orenstein would distribute a piece of challa or cake to each person so that they would have something to eat when they woke up on Shabbos morning. Shabbos in Apt really was a special day. No one had to worry about his next meal and everyone was far removed from everyday life.

Chapter Three

Lifecycle Events and the Greatest *Simcha*

Births in Apt – especially in *cheder* if the baby was a boy – were a source of much excitement. The boys knew from experience that a special treat was in store, involving a trip to the home of the newborn. Escorted by the boys' rebbe, the children would enter the home and recite *Shema* and *HaMalach HaGoel* for the sake of the baby's well-being prior to the *bris.*

Then the baby's mother or grandmother would distribute sweets to all the little boys. Salek's classmates raised both of their hands to try and acquire a double portion. Some children succeeded in landing two sweets, depriving a classmate, who would cry at this great injustice.

Alas, tears and sobs were of no avail and the boys showed no mercy. The anguish of those who missed out was heightened when the sweets were unwrapped. The lucky ones compared their booty while the others looked on in envy.

Although Salek was only four years old when his younger sister was born, he remembered every detail of the birth. He had been playing calmly when out of nowhere a neighbor ran in and told Nacha Ella to lie down. She then rushed off to call the midwife who lived close to the shul. The woman, with ruddy cheeks and a sturdy build, was born into the profession, as her mother was also a midwife.

The first thing the midwife did was boil water and see to it that Nacha Ella was comfortably situated on the bed yet easily accessible. Hershel was out of town at the time, but this was compensated for by the presence of the midwife's mother, a gray-haired lady with long earrings who was of great reassurance to Nacha Ella.

Salek took up his post in the kitchen, once again demonstrating his serendipitous ability to be in the right place whenever something exciting was occurring. The midwives remained all night long and the baby was born in the early hours of the morning.

That very morning Hershel returned home from the countryside. He went to shul, received an *aliya,* and named the little girl Shifra Leah. Everyone was joyful and excited to welcome another child into the Orenstein family.

Before she left, the senior midwife cleared the kitchen table and began to tear up old sheets into big squares to be used as diapers. Salek, who never missed a beat, peeped through a small crack in the door and watched the midwives wrapping and binding his baby sister to make sure that she would not have crooked feet.

***

Salek and the youth of Apt were also exposed to the other extreme of the life cycle, having witnessed many funeral processions. Apt and its environs was bereft of a hospital, a clinic, and even a doctor. People were born in bed, and that was usually where they died. Some were fortunate and could afford the village healer, called a *felcher,* who claimed to be able to cure the sick with herbs.

Funerals were a source of fascination to the curious children. There were no coffins, only a stretcher that was covered with a black sheet. The mourners, following the wagon, led the procession to the graveyard.

The women would wail hysterically, inconsolably digging their nails into their faces until they bled. In abject grief they mourned their dear husbands, parents, siblings, or children.

The only time Salek ever went to the cemetery was when his grandfather passed away. That was the first time he saw how they buried the dead and noticed the *chevra kaddisha* placing two pieces of earthenware over the deceased's eyes.

Salek learned early that tragedy was not a private, discreet affair in Apt. He was about twelve years old when the doors of the *yeshiva ketana* suddenly flew open. A woman and her children burst in and ran straight for the *aron kodesh*. The distraught woman almost ripped down the *paroches* in her struggle to open the *aron*, whereupon she fell to the floor crying, pleading for her husband's recovery.

The scene shocked Salek and broke his heart. The woman, like many others, could not read Hebrew, so she couldn't properly pray. Instead, she cried out in Yiddish, "I am not leaving this place until You promise me that my husband will have a *refua shelema*!"

The *shammes* approached the grief-stricken woman and attempted to offer some words of comfort. The rabbi joined in the consolation and asked for her husband's name and the name of his mother, promising that he would make a *mi sheberach* for his recovery. When she had received these assurances, she composed herself and returned home.

Salek was disturbed by what he had just witnessed, and it was impossible for him to concentrate any longer on his studies. All he could think of was what would happen to him if harm befell his parents?

***

The *shtetl* of Apt came to life early every weekday morning when the men would arise and rush to one of the houses of prayer, better known as *shtieblach*. Every segment of society, from the most affluent (there weren't very many of those) to the woodcutters, would all congregate in the *shtiebel* and plead with the Almighty to send them a better day.

There were some who came to express their joy and give thanks, and many others who came to pour out their sorrows. Some clapped their hands Heavenwards others shook their bodies in every direction, attempting – or so it seemed – to bring the Heavens down to earth.

In the very center of Apt was the Great Synagogue, primarily attended by the working class. This majestic building, with stained glass windows and a domed roof, had an intricately hand-painted ceiling portraying each of the twelve constellations that corresponded to the months of the year. The shul also boasted a *chazan* and a choir.

One of Salek's friends was the premier singer of the shul choir.[4] But the Orensteins had nothing to do with the Great Synagogue, as they were members of the Gerrer *shtiebel* – a modest wooden building that paled in comparison to its Aptian neighbor. The *shteibel*'s attendees were decidedly hasidic in their lifestyle and attire. The men wore *kapotehs* and silken *bekishehs* on Shabbos, although only a few sported *shtreimelach*. The *shtreimelach* wearers were either elderly individuals or newlyweds who wished to advertise that they had married into an affluent family. Salek wore a *gartel* from the age of five.

4. Salek would never learn how truly beautiful his voice was until years – and a lifetime – later when the two of them were subjected to forced labor in a quarry. In the midst of that torture, as they slaved all day toward their own ruination, this friend's voice rang out and echoed amid the rocks.

Salek's grandfather was seated in a most prominent position in the *shtiebel,* adjacent to the *aron kodesh.* Despite his advanced age he would stand all day long on Rosh HaShana and Yom Kippur.

On Yom Kippur, the *shtiebel* was filled with memorial candles, two to three feet tall, that were sunk into the sand to keep them steady. The non-Jew who worked for the Orensteins was hired to stand outside the door of the shul, in case one of the candles fell over. Because the Gerrer *shtiebel* was a wooden structure it could easily burn down.

The *shammes* of the *beis midrash* was privy to all of the events in town and he loved to share his scoops with Salek. When the *shammes* wasn't spreading news, his job – in the winter — was to clean and stoke the stove so that the *beis midrash* would be warm and comfortable.

But even then, work could not prevent Apt's raconteur from sharing the story of why the fireplace's iron rod was in two pieces.

The only way to exit Apt to the west toward the large town of Ostrowiec was by crossing the river. The problem was that the bridge, according to the lore of Apt, was infested with *shedim* (demons). The Jews of Apt feared them greatly and it became impossible to cross over the bridge. The situation became so unbearable that a famous rabbi decided to take matters into his own hands, quite literally, and had the iron rod that the *shammes* had so proudly displayed commissioned to use in battle against the *shedim.*

With tremendous bravery, the rabbi brazenly trod upon the bridge and was attacked, quite naturally, by the *shedim.* Alas, the demons were not adequately demonic for the rabbi, who fiercely battled them, breaking the solid iron rod in the process. It was a small price to pay to clear the bridge of *shedim* and open the way from Apt to Ostrowiec.

But like the law of matter, the *shammes* continued, the *shedim* merely relocated – to no other place than Apt's *beis midrash*! They made it impossible to learn at night. Obviously, nothing was holy to these *shedim,* and they would remove the men's *shtreimelach,* blow out the lights, and perpetrate other forms of mischief, until the very same "*shedim* courageous" rabbi appeared and threatened them with another attack.

***

Purim was traditionally the time when the rabbi was acknowledged for his services by Apt's residents via *mishloach manot.* Salek would deliver the Orensteins' gift, consisting of his father's homemade wine and mother's homemade cakes and *hamantaschen* that were at least four inches wide, together with a couple of apples or whatever fruit was in season.

Salek was delighted that it was his lot to deliver the *mishloach manot* to the rabbi. The rebbetzin would present him with one of her little challos and a handful of chickpeas wrapped in a twist of paper. Salek loved those little salty *arbes* so much that by the time he reached home, there were hardly any left.

***

When he wasn't teaching, Reb Shloimaleh, Salek's instructor, would learn in the home of Zucker, one of Apt's wealthiest Jews. Zucker was a very pious individual who had not been blessed with children but was endowed with a generous spirit.

When Zucker decided to commission the writing of a *sefer Torah* the news spread like wildfire and generated more excitement than Apt had known for decades. Even in Torah-saturated Apt this was a very uncommon event, as so few could afford such an expensive mitzva.

One day the *shammes* (who was Salek's steady source of information) revealed that the *sefer Torah* had been completed and that Zucker was going to host a feast for the entire town. Not another word was necessary, and school was dropped for the day from Salek's agenda.

The eager lad posted himself outside Zucker's house so that he would have a firsthand view of the goings-on, and he didn't miss a beat… or a bang. Out of nowhere the pounding of drums could be heard as the *klezmer* troupe advanced toward the Zucker home.

Among the *klezmorim* Salek saw Chazkel, his music teacher, merrily sawing at his violin. Salek now had all the connections he needed for a front-row seat, and he moved up to the center of the action. A group of little boys, *klezmer*-wannabes, showed up clanging on saucepans with sticks.

The *klezmerim* were followed by a parade of six elaborately decorated horses, whose riders were holding flaming torches aloft. The horsemen were leading the way for the *chuppa* that was proudly held tall above the *sefer Torah* itself. The townsfolk struggled to get near and kiss it.

The crowds thronged through the narrow streets, some of them no wider than a dining room table. Inching its way gingerly forward to the tune of resounding, joyous singing, the *sefer Torah*, decked in ornate silver ornaments, arrived at its new home, Apt's Great Synagogue. Under normal circumstances the walk from the Zucker home to the synagogue would take no more than five minutes. With all of the fanfare, the procession took almost two hours!

And that was just the beginning. Once the crowd entered the shul, things really started happening! There was so much dancing and so many *hakafos* that everyone's clothing was wringing wet from perspiration and their faces resembled Reb Hershel's in the *mikve*'s steam room.

The *chazan* totally stole the show. A short man with a giant voice, he knew this was his day in the sun, and he performed non-stop. He was attired in his Yom Kippur finery, bellowing "*vayehi binsoa ha'aron,*" supported by a full choir.

On that day Salek was jealous that he was not one of the choirboys – but he was hardly eligible. The issue was not his voice but engaging in an activity that was deemed utterly non-hasidic, something that his father would never sanction.

When the goings-on in the shul were finally over, Zucker hosted a private, lavish *seuda* for invited guests. But true to character, Zucker also had several tables set up in the shul yard for the poor folk of Apt. Each one was laden with challos, cakes, confectioneries, and a varied spread that pleased the needy, who grabbed whatever they could lay their hands on. Salek maintained that it was the greatest *simcha* he had ever seen.

Chapter Four

First Shadows

One early Friday morning in September 1939, Apt was awoken to the shrill noise of a siren. The primitive, pump-action siren could be operated only by a town council official, and it was effective in rousing the townsfolk and propelling them to the market square to learn that Germany had invaded Poland.

Although everyone was very perturbed by the news, there was a measure of consolation in the fact that it would be months, according to their calculations, before the war reached Apt. Then the second siren sounded.

At lunchtime two Luftwaffe planes swooped down so low that Salek could see the pilot's expressions and how unfazed they appeared to be by the pathetic gunshots fired by a Polish policeman.

For fear of an imminent German incursion, the Orensteins took cover in the cellar of their building. This meant crowding into a dirty, rubbish-infested hole in the ground with five other families. There was scarcely enough room to breathe, the stench was overpowering, and rats scampered across the earthen floor. The little children wept.

When the Orensteins emerged from their shelter at nightfall it was already Shabbos, and they set about blacking out their windows with blankets. Unable to make the proper preparations, the Shabbos meal was extremely modest, and the fact that no one had a chance to bathe contributed to the downcast atmosphere. Salek's blanket was conscripted to cover the window, so he had to sleep beneath a coat.

The residents of Apt awoke the next morning to a town that had been plastered with emergency posters. They attended shul as usual, but the circumstances caused major distraction and anxiety. The siren went on and off throughout the day, repeatedly sending the Orensteins down to their dismal shelter. The conditions in the cellar began to deteriorate steadily, with dirty water from the rusty pipes in the floor above seeping through the ceiling.

On Sunday, Salek accompanied his father to the stables, where the horses had been deprived of food and drink for two days. The second his father opened the barn door the horses charged out to the nearby river. The dogs, who also lived in the stables and who by then were very weak, were fed some of the leftovers from Shabbos.

While at the stables, which were located outside of Apt proper, Salek could see Polish soldiers on the march. It was not an impressive sight. They were a ragtag band of conscripts whose vintage rifles were slung over their shoulders with string.

Hershel Orenstein was concerned that he might be drafted, since he was only in his forties. He was equally concerned about the well-being of his brothers, neither of whom lived in Apt.

Hershel had an advantage over the other residents of Apt when it came to acquiring information. His business possessed a telephone whose phone number was the single digit, "2"; number "1" belonged to the mayor. The contraption looked like a wooden box with a handle sticking out of its side that had to be cranked in order to function.

Through a telephone exchange Hershel was able to determine that his brother in Ostrowiec, whom Salek had only met once, had been conscripted. Telephone and all, he was unable to establish contact with his other brother.

Every day new posters appeared in town, and it was the windows of the Jewish shops that were always plastered with the notices.

On Monday, the fourth day of the war, the Germans – who were still reported to be months away – arrived. Hershel's wheat stores were attacked from the air, leaving half a dozen horses dead or bleeding. The damage was extensive, and the Polish infantry, perhaps the main target, was also slaughtered on their march toward the east.

At the same time a fire broke out in the part of town where Salek's grandfather Avrohom Orenstein lived. This event provided Salek with his first opportunity to observe Apt's voluntary fire department in action. Their equipment consisted of a red and yellow wagon with two ladders on the sides and a big barrel in the center holding two hoses.

The wagon was drawn by the firefighters themselves, who wore dark blue uniforms and strange, pointed helmets. When a fire erupted out of town, the funny-looking volunteers rushed into Hershel's stables to borrow horses for the wagon. Every time the same procedure was followed, but it was always an exercise in futility, for by the time the emergency wagon arrived at the scene of a fire there was never anything left to save.

Along with the Polish army, large numbers of civilians were fleeing their towns and villages in the direction of the Russian border. Some passed through Apt seeking water and supplies for their long journey.

In a matter of days there would be nothing left to give them. Bakeries were running short of flour, the fruit and vegetable growers were reluctant to come into town to sell their produce, and some of the regular traders, upon whom everyone depended for food, had been recruited to the army. Money also ran short.

The Jewish Council of Apt (of which Hershel Orenstein was a member) set up a soup kitchen outside the Great Synagogue to attempt to alleviate the hunger. Hershel called in favors from all of his business contacts to try to acquire food for the Jews of Apt.

Although his personal grain stores had been damaged in the bombing raid, the family managed to salvage some of the wheat and were assiduously looking for a way to convert it to flour. Necessity is the mother of invention, and in that spirit a hand-operated mincing machine was eventually located to grind the wheat. From that point on, any bread that the Orensteins consumed was made from flour that they had milled themselves. Salek was put in charge of the wheat-milling operation.

Difficulty, like necessity, fosters creativity, and the Orenstein team became very resourceful. They figured out that if they were to boil the small brown seeds that abounded in the area – but had never been awarded any attention in the past – and then crush them, a smidgen of oil could be extracted for cooking. The result was a long way from conventional cooking oil, but altogether, conditions were a long, long way from conventional.

On Wednesday, the sixth day of the invasion, Salek went to the marketplace to check on developments. The place was deserted. He was just about to leave when he heard a continuous, mechanical, rattling noise that grew louder by the second. Suddenly Salek saw an apparition far more demonic than any *shedim* that the famous *shedim*-fighting rabbi ever had to contend with!

The young boy had never seen a tank before, and the vision was more ghastly and dreadful than anything he had ever seen or imagined. Salek froze on the spot, his hands clasped behind his back. A German soldier jumped down and shouted, "*Was hast du?* What have you got?," assuming Salek was concealing a weapon.

Salek raised his empty hands. The soldier then barked, "*Wo ist die Hauptsdadt?* Where is the capital?" but the lad was too terrified to open his mouth. He ran as fast as his legs would carry him to his family's cellar where his parents were hiding. Salek's parents had been petrified over his well-being in his absence, but when he revealed to them what he had experienced it did little to calm their nerves.

That evening, for the first time since the war broke out, there was finally illumination in Apt. The pitch darkness from the previous week was replaced with bright light as the German army set fire to an entire street of shops and houses to light their way through town.

The Germans settled themselves into two local schools and began to issue orders, including a strict curfew and a prohibition against storing any food. The punishment for violating these, or any Nazi edicts, was death. All food had to be submitted to the Germans. Jews were required to wear yellow armbands. Hershel, Salek's father, had heard how the Germans delighted in tearing the beards out of Jewish faces, so he took the precaution of trimming his beard very close to his face.

On the heels of the German invaders arrived a large number of Poles with swastika armbands, claiming to be *Volksdeutsche,* of German ancestry. Their claim was patently absurd, as these supposed *Volksdeutsche* could not speak a word of German. Still, they excelled at persecuting and attacking the Jews, which made up for their fallacious lineage.

Elsewhere in Poland, Jews would be forced into ghettos. For all intents and purposes, Apt was already a ghetto before the formal order of ghettoization was issued. Hershel Orenstein somberly informed his family of the order that any Jews living in and around the marketplace must vacate their property.

The Orenstein furniture was superb by Apt's standards, and Hershel therefore arranged for the large items to be loaded onto wagons and delivered to one of his Polish business associates in the countryside for safekeeping. There were no allusions that they would be able to transport their furniture to where they were headed. Furthermore, Hershel thought that it would be prudent to have something set aside in the hope that they would survive.

There was very little room in the new Orenstein quarters, especially after the family was joined by Salek's maternal grandmother. Their new "home" consisted of conditions that were crowded, dirty, cold, and depressing. There was no flooring, just trodden earth upon which Nacha Ella sprinkled as much sawdust as she could gather from the yard to cover the ground. Salek's parents slept on a shelf without a mattress. Salek and his brother, Yehuda Fischel, slept on sacks filled with straw, while their elder sister Pola slept with their grandmother and little Shifra Leah slept near their mother.

In the morning, the sacks were removed and placed outside in the yard to enable a little maneuvering room. The only available facility was an extremely primitive outhouse which was merely a ditch that afforded no possibility of sitting down. Needless to say, paper could not to be found, aside from a few scraps Hershel managed to bring back from the *Judenrat,* the Jewish council the Nazis imposed on the people to fulfill their will. The *mikve* was sealed, and there was no way to bathe or maintain even the most minimal hygiene.

All of the barns were used by the Germans to store their food supplies. Every farmer was required to submit produce, for which he received payment in worthless zlotys. Hershel Orenstein was in charge of managing the stores and seeing to it that they remained locked. If anyone dared remove a scrap of food from these stores they would be killed immediately. Even dauntless Salek did not brave it.

Because Hershel was so useful to the Germans in overseeing the food stores he was awarded a few special privileges — all connected to his work — such as being allowed past the town gates. He used these opportunities to acquire small amounts of grain through his connections in the country. Salek was able to grind these paltry amounts of grain into flour, which was then kneaded into dough and brought to the baker, who took a portion for himself in lieu of payment. The resultant measly loaf had to last all week. Yet at least they had something to eat and knew that they were better off than many others.

Chapter Five

Liquidation of the Jewish Community in Opatow

The necessities of the Jews were completely ignored by the Nazi conquerors. Nor were they permitted to express their needs. Their only method of communication was via the *Judenrat,* the Jewish council, which was created exclusively to serve the dictates of the Germans. Hence the voice of the Jews was muffled and gagged.

The first assignment of Apt's *Judenrat* was to clear the roads of any obstructions in preparation for broadening and fortifying the streets. The Polish roads were no more than two narrow, trodden tracks, and the Germans had to provide for their mechanized army, which would require wide lanes with a hard bed underneath.

Time was of the essence. The rainy season had already commenced and winter was around the corner. It was imperative that the Germans complete the project before the tanks got stuck in terrain that they could not negotiate. After all, their ultimate goal was obviously not Apt, but Moscow.

The *Judenrat* was forced to provide Jewish youth between the ages of twelve and fourteen to clear the streets, and one hundred laborers to work in the quarry, hammering stones to pave the roads. Salek's brother was among those selected to slave in the quarry that was three miles away. Salek helped his grandmother in her shop, as a limited amount of trading was still permitted. After a while, it was decided that Salek's older brother would be of greater benefit in the shop, and the brothers' roles were exchanged.

Salek had a large hammer for breaking the rocks and a smaller hammer for smashing them into two-inch squares. The finished products were piled into heaps that were supposed to be of a specific height; every day the workers were expected to produce a standard measure three feet high.

It was a full day's work that began early in the morning and was not completed before evening. The *Volksdeutsche* overseers would verify the height of the pile, and if they were not satisfied the worker would have to remain behind until the quota was met. The stones were transported by non-Jewish wagon drivers to the roads, where they were pressed into the earth to form a gravel bed that was later covered with asphalt.

Every morning Salek discovered mounds of the previous day's stones abandoned throughout the quarry. Cleverly, he would station himself beside one of those accumulations. No one was aware of his head start, and the industrious young boy was known as the best worker in the quarry. *A nechtiger tug!*

Over the course of time, it became more difficult to continue the deception, especially as he realized that he wasn't cheating the Germans as much as his fellow Jew who had slaved all day to produce Salek's "start-up." Salek therefore developed other strategies to ease his day, such as concealing large rocks at the bottom of his pile and producing only enough small stones to give the appearance of a complete pile.

Aside from quarry and road work, Jews were a disposable workforce that was assigned to other arduous, grueling, monotonous, and dangerous tasks. Salek was next assigned to be a water carrier for the German army's field kitchen.

The great advantage to this chore was that it enabled him to steal potatoes and slip them into his trousers – always remembering to tie the leg ends first. Salek looked thoroughly comical until he hit upon the solution of wearing larger trousers.

The *Wehrmacht* presence in Apt was bearable – just – until Ukrainians joined their ranks. These collaborators wished to convince the Germans how committed they were to their mutual cause and spared no effort oppressing the Jews. Men and women, young and old, were constantly beaten and left half-dead on the streets.

***

One winter evening after curfew, Salek and his cousin snuck over to the stables in order to feed the horses, who had been locked up for over a day and were frightfully cold and hungry. Salek suggested harnessing the horses to the sleigh so that the exertion would warm them up.

The cousins first rode to the river to enable the horses to drink and then galloped around the field. Suddenly two soldiers appeared, looked at their watches, and confirmed that it was past curfew. "Do you know where the cemetery is?" they barked at Salek.

Salek, too scared to move, could not open his mouth. The Germans jumped onto the sleigh and commanded that they be taken to headquarters, which was surrounded by high hedges on all sides. The soldiers got off and ordered the boys to wait for them.

It suddenly occurred to Salek that there could be only one reason for asking the way to the cemetery. Why should the Germans inconvenience themselves by dragging away corpses? It would be so much more efficient to deliver the offenders to the cemetery live.

Salek took hold of the reins, whipped the horses like fury, and drove the horses and the sleigh up and over the high hedge. With his heart pounding and the taste of bile piercing his tongue, the lad did not even look over his shoulder until he reached the stable and firmly bolted the door.

By the time the Germans came searching for the boys and their horses, they had long returned to their homes and frightened families. Salek's parents were horror-stricken, but none of their entreaties could get their son to reveal what had transpired.

The next morning, Salek's father returned home from the *Judenrat* ashen faced. German security, known as the *Sicherheitsdienst,* reported that two Jewish boys had disobeyed orders and had been caught sleighing the previous night. The *Sicherheitsdienst* demanded that the offenders be handed over or there would be a mass, collective price to pay.

Salek did not say a word.

The head of the *Judenrat* explained to the German commander that the offending boys could not have been Jews; no Jew would ever have the temerity to do such a thing. The matter was uncharacteristically dropped by the Nazis; but the experience did not stop Salek from going down to the stables to feed the horses.

One day, as Salek again headed to the stable, he heard a voice in Yiddish beckoning from over the church wall. The Germans housed all their prisoners in the church compound. "*Yingel*!" came the desperate whisper. "Go home and get me trousers and a jacket." This would enable a key disguise for the prisoner's getaway after he jumped over the wall.

The idea of assisting a fellow Jew escape from the Nazis greatly appealed to the boy, and he raced to his *zeide*'s house, took whatever clothing he could lay his hands on, and brought it to the stable. Salek then returned to the rendezvous point and placed a strong box at the foot of the high church wall to break the prisoner's fall. Seconds later a Nazi noticed the box and cursed, "Damn Poles! They leave their rubbish everywhere." Still, the soldier did nothing to remove it.

When the sentry within the compound went to patrol the far wall, the Yiddish-speaking prisoner leaped up and over, continuing on to the Orenstein stable, where he changed into the clothing that Salek had prepared. He instructed the boy to burn his prisoner's uniform to eliminate any evidence.

After the execution of this escape, Salek returned to the church wall, where other voices called out to him in Yiddish. The same successful method was again employed, with each escapee availing themselves of the secret stash of getaway clothing in the stable. In the course of that one day, he helped four individuals escape. As far as Salek was concerned, these bold acts marked the end of his childhood.

One day a sentry caught Salek next to the forbidden church wall. Fortunately, he was not helping anyone escape at that moment, but his sheer proximity was an offense. "*Was machst du so nahe zu den Kriegsgefangenen*? What are you doing so close to the prisoners?" the Nazi demanded. "I'm just, just…just looking for cigarettes," Salek stuttered.

"Well, you won't find any here!" the Nazi replied gruffly.

Less than two weeks later, whoever remained in the church compound was shot. Salek had spared no effort to ensure that no Yiddish-speaker remained.

Because of Hershel's relative freedom, Salek wondered why his father never attempted to disguise the family as Polish peasants who could have been smuggled over the Hungarian border. Obviously, there was a risk involved, but it paled in comparison to the fate of Aptian Jewry: massacre.

The signs of what lay ahead were manifest as the situation constantly worsened. Two Jews attempting to escape were shot, as were two women found with unauthorized grain. Edict followed edict. The *Judenrat* was to supply two hundred youngsters between the ages of six and twenty-five to build concentration camps.

As Hershel was relatively influential, the Orensteins were spared the first selection. Weeks went by, and nothing was ever heard again from these youngsters.

One day, as Salek was walking up from the stores, he heard gunshots. What happened next occurred in a flash: Nazis with their Polish *Volksdeutschen* allies surrounded the town, shouting, "*Juden heraus!* Jews out!" as they shot into the air. People rushed out of their houses in total pandemonium. A dozen open trucks awaited them in the main street.

All of the males were ordered on board the trucks, and any individual who had difficulty climbing up was swiftly eliminated. Among the captured was Salek, who saw his father gazing down in sheer horror from the first-floor window of the *Judenrat* building. Hershel's hat was off and both his hands were clasping his face in despair at the sight of his young son being led away.

That was the very last time Salek saw his father. He would also never see his mother again.

Chapter Six

Road to Hell on Earth

There were nearly fifty individuals crammed into the truck with Salek and it was impossible to move, let alone sit down. Although it was Salek's first-ever ride on a motorized vehicle, the thrill was lost in the agony.

Salek looked desperately for signposts along the way to determine where they were headed. Throughout the ride bullets were fired over their heads, and hardly anyone spoke. Deep, mournful sobbing echoed among the despairing passengers, who had no idea where they were going. All Salek knew was that wherever it was, he was going to run away!

About five hours later the captives arrived at an ammunition factory. The relief of leaving the truck, which was a pool of urine, was extremely short-lived. They were brought to the *Appelplatz* (area for roll call) where they were given a typical welcome for Jewish prisoners. A barrage of shouting was directed at them: "*Schnell! Ihr verfluchte Juden! Wo seit ihr jetzt? In der Synagogue?* Quick! You cursed Jews! Where are you now? In the Synagogue?"

Men dressed in white gowns inspected the prisoners with penetrating, hate-filled eyes. The arrivals were divided into groups and marched off to either *Werk* A or *Werk* B. Salek was sent to *Werk* B, which was about three miles away, and placed under the command of taskmasters known as the *Werkschutz*. They were a motley crew of illiterate, unkempt felons and murderers who were released from prison by the Germans in exchange for their services.

The *Werkschutz* were mostly Ukrainians, and they gave orders in a hodgepodge of German, Ukrainian, and Polish. These uncivilized brutes sought nothing more than food, shelter, and the opportunity to murder Jews. All of them carried guns with fixed bayonets.

As the prisoners hadn't eaten anything since their capture in Apt they were in a terrible state. Naturally it was difficult for the exhausted individuals to stand in line, and when one veered out of the formation he was shot.

There were three fences which surrounded the quarters, and each was electrified and patrolled by vicious, wolflike dogs.

Upon arrival to *Werk* B an attractive Jewish blonde named Helena, who held an administrative position in the camp, addressed the prisoners in Polish. They were under the rule of the sectional director, Herr Skladowski, she explained, who controlled all of the loading and unloading of the vehicles that entered the munitions compound.

The man was five feet tall with a hunchback, and rumor had it that Helena was Skladowski's mistress. Any uneducated Jew could speak German far better than Skladowski, who corralled the first twenty Jews he saw, including Salek, for a labor battalion.

These twenty were taken to yet a different camp that housed four barracks. On the left was a barrack with a long trench within; this was the latrine. And even though it was eight hours since Salek had left Apt, he still could not bring himself to use such horrendous facilities.

The bunks had the appearance of having been hastily erected the day before. Everyone was ordered to grab some straw to serve as bedding.

Later that night, two boys brought in a large container of soup. The prisoners grabbed a crude tin, as there were no spoons or cutlery to speak of, and stood in line. When it was Salek's turn and he got a peek of the soup, he was overcome with nausea. Floating on the surface were some whitish-yellow pieces of flesh, and despite his incredible hunger he could not ingest such manifestly unkosher items as horsemeat or rat flesh.

He settled instead for some water that was available from a tap and was consoled by his cousin Avram, a distant cousin from his father's side, who had also been captured and incarcerated in Skarzysko. Avram, who was a little bit older and had already started high school, assured him that the *Judenrat* would surely send food parcels. Avram used to live in Lodz, but when it was taken over by the Germans, he moved to Opatow thinking it would be easier to survive there.

At 5:30 the next morning the savage Ukrainians banged on the door, warning that there was less than a minute to get up and out of the barrack. Truthfully, it was not a long procedure, since no one had to get dressed. The prisoners only had to put on their shoes, which they had been warned to place under their heads so that they would not be stolen during the night.

In the *Appelplatz* the prisoners were lined up and given a measure of black water that was called "coffee." This was followed by lining up for the daily ration of bread. Salek discovered that the best slice was from the ends. However, over time he noticed that the slice that was once usually one inch thick shrunk to three-quarters of an inch and then to just half an inch. Those in charge of distributing the bread wished to be sure that plenty would be left for themselves. Their slices grew thicker and thicker while the others' slices were gradually reduced to crumbs.

After twenty-four hours at the Skarzysko-Kamienna slave labor camp, Salek assessed his new reality. He was all by himself without parents or siblings, penniless, hungry, and with nothing to wear but the shirt on his back. His only remaining family connection was with Avram. Exacerbating the sense of despair was the vile hunchback Skladowski and his Jewish overseers.

The first day's roll-call was convened for Skladowski to make yet another selection. When he did this, he never approached the prisoner face-to-face but by sneaking around so that you could not see him coming. Skladowski never even had to open his mouth. When he settled upon a candidate, he would slap him with his truncheon to indicate "selection." Since no one could see him, it was impossible to tell where the stick would fall next, and the tension was palpable.

Salek received a slap from behind and a Jewish overseer called him out of the row. Salek was assigned to the raw material division. His first job was to unload heavy boxes filled with metal cups that were to be repurposed into ammunition. The work was back-breaking, even by quarry standards.

It took four workers to unload just one box! The strain and exertion generated tremendous thirst, but they were not allowed to slake their parched lips until one o'clock when soup was distributed.

Salek's initial abhorrence for the soup was displaced by extreme hunger, which is what made him so curious as to why the veteran prisoners did not race forward when the food was served. Salek discovered that the veterans, just as famished as everyone else, waited until right before the end when the soup collected at the bottom was at its thickest.

After the meager rations it was back to work. There weren't any hand carts or machines to transfer the heavy boxes from the railway track to the storage depots. Like mules and oxen, the emaciated prisoners were forced to haul exceedingly heavy loads.

The first box was the easiest, as it could be deposited on the warehouse floor without being stacked. But as the day wore on the prisoners had to pile one box upon another, which was an impossible strain. Overseeing the transfer were the trigger-happy *werkschutz,* whose truncheons were in constant motion, cracking skulls and breaking backs. Their nonstop shouts, in a mixture of Ukrainian and Polish with a tad of German thrown in, echoed in the cold warehouse. The guards worked in three-hour shifts, which meant that the taskmasters switched several times a day, and each fresh shift would not tolerate the slightest delay.

Often, by the end of his shift, Salek was so worn out that he was physically incapable of standing in the soup line. There were times that he even missed his bread allocation. When he later begged for what he deserved they snarled, "You're lying. You already had your bread!"

After the group worked for several days in the transport division, new prisoners arrived to build up the workforce, and as a result Salek was redeployed to the railway platform. There were dozens of cars there filled with coal that had to be unloaded. The coal in those wagons was nothing like the neat, tidy nuggets coal consumers are familiar with. The train contained coal dregs – the poorest of the poor – just fragments and thin dust. In no time, anyone working at this job was thoroughly covered in coal dust. The coal was loaded onto wheelbarrows and brought to the coal bunkers.

Just as Salek's instinctive dislike of food that was neither kosher nor fit for human consumption was rapidly disappearing, so too were any remnants of his pampered nature or refined habits that he had brought from home. Otherwise, there was no way to continue to the future.

After Salek's first day on the coal unit he was confronted with what seemed to be an insurmountable dilemma. How could he wash himself without soap or hot water? Cold water was available in the yard, but that could never remove the oily coal dust from every part of his body.

Observing his struggle, other inmates suggested that he steal some bicarbonate crystals to help remove the greasy dirt. The substance was scattered on the floor of the ammunition factory to soak up leaking machine oil.

When the first opportunity arose, Salek grabbed as many soda crystals as he could. He then washed himself, vigorously rubbing the grains all over his body. The pain from the acidic material penetrating his skin was excruciating and resulted in a dreadful rash all over his body and bizarre swellings on his face.

"Oh!" the inmates said when they saw him. "You've used too much!"

Thankfully, Salek was transferred from the coal detachment to unloading timber. The camp was close to a forest and trees were felled nearby. The work area had been carefully cordoned off and supplied with vicious Alsatian tracking dogs to prevent any of the workforce from fleeing. The idea of escape never left Salek's mind, particularly when he was working close to the railway tracks, which were wide open. The sentry on guard in that area, however, was very alert, preventing the actualization of this plan.

One morning the prisoners were assembled to an unusual *appel* attended by two SS officers named Stein and Herring, who were both heads of departments. Rumor had it that Stein, who was responsible for antiaircraft cannons, was not as cruel as Herring, who produced bullets.

Herring had a wandering eye and his reputation as a sadist was legendary. He operated a strict quota system that mandated that a certain number of bullets had to be produced each day, no matter what. If the quotas were not met, the Jewish supervisors were the first to pay the price. Accordingly, his workforce was oppressed and denied food until the right number of bullets was manufactured.

From this *appel* Herring chose twenty boys, Salek included. Salek was assigned to work the *blei* machine, which filled bullets with lead. The lead that was fed into the machine came in long coils that were heavily coated with grease to prevent rust.

Each time Salek had to maneuver the coil he struggled with the grease, which invariably covered him. This resulted in an agonizing skin rash. His clothing, the same set of clothes that he had worn since arriving from Apt, no longer afforded any protection. They had gaping holes and were in tatters. Salek did what he could to mend the biggest holes by "sewing" them with wire.

The overseer for this factory was a non-Jew who had worked for the Polish government on the premises before the war. This man always wanted to know what Salek's father did and whether he had any hidden money. If Salek would reveal to him the whereabouts of a hidden treasure he would reciprocate with food. But when Salek informed him that Hershel didn't have any money nor did he know what his parents did with the little that they had, he blamed the poor boy for whatever went wrong.

Salek was assigned to the night shifts, which meant he slaved until six or seven in the morning. By that point he could stay awake no longer and it took the greatest resolve to even collect the so-called "coffee" before collapsing in his barrack.

Sleeping right next to Salek in the barrack was his distant cousin Avram. Salek looked up to his cousin, who was a source of encouragement for him.

One morning Salek tried to wake Avram but he could not get him to stir. "You're late for work," Salek prodded. In desperation Salek turned to an elderly man (by camp standards, thirty was considered elderly) for advice.

The man leaned over near Avram's face: no breath. He placed his head against his heart: no heartbeat. The prognosis was clear. Salek went over to the block *fuhrer* and reported that his cousin was dead. The body was taken outside but there was no sheet or blanket, nothing to cover him. This was the first instance of a natural death in the camp.

Prisoners were summoned to bury the body. Salek and two others went out to the woods with a pick and some shovels and stopped where the *werkschutz* ordered the grave be dug. The earth was rock solid because of the winter, and every inch of headway they made was set back by the many knotted tree roots which crisscrossed beneath the earth's surface.

Salek attempted to pull up a tree root, and in his struggle he lobbed off a sizable portion of his thumb, spouting blood all over the snow. Salek held onto his thumb as tightly as he could to try and stem the bleeding, simultaneously burying his cousin. Under the muzzles of the *werkschutz* there was never time off for an injury.

Avram was deprived of a proper burial with interment deep in the ground, but the men tried their best. Salek pondered how unfortunate it was to be buried in the middle of a forest in an unmarked grave. Even his *yahrzeit* was a mystery. Salek no longer knew the specific date or even the month, only that it was winter.

Still, it was the first natural death in the camp, and many, indeed most, were jealous of the deceased. In the macabre world of the slave labor camp it was a rare blessing not to die from a bullet to the skull, and an even more remarkable blessing not to be forced to dig your own grave, not to mention being shot but not fatally and expiring in exquisite agony hours or days later…

Returning to the camp, an older enlisted man commented with certainty, "You will survive, for you buried yourself with your cousin today when your blood went into his grave."

The statement gave Salek pause and seemed to make sense. Conditions at Skarzysko made death inevitable, but now that his blood had descended into the earth, it was as if he was already buried. And you can't be buried twice!

From the time of Avram's passing not a word was heard from any of Apt's Jewish residents. The silence was not accidental. The Jews had been marched off in the direction of Ostrowiec where they boarded trains, destination:

Treblinka.

For reasons that Salek never understood, he was moved off the *blei* machine and onto the *hilze* machine, which made bullet casings. This was a definite improvement; the casings just flew right off the press without grease, filth, or a struggle.

Supervision was a different matter. The German woman in charge, Hilda, was built like a beast, acted like a beast, and her face resembled a gorilla. She marched back and forth inspecting the size of the casings and monitoring the quality of work.

As daunting as Hilda was, the new assignment was far easier and cleaner than the *blei* machine. Salek was desperate not to go back to that dreaded work, so he applied himself to the new job. Indeed, he worked so assiduously at his new machine that one day "Hilda the Beast" appeared and began to curse and swear like any of her male counterparts.

"From now on," Hilda snarled, "you are in charge of all these machines!" She found Salek's work to be nearly impeccable, which was crucial. If the bullets were not precise, the guns would jam. And so Salek labored on, night after night, producing bullets so the German Army would be able to murder more Jews.

Chapter Seven

A Very Narrow Escape from Death

One morning, just as Salek was closing his eyes, he heard shouts of "*Raus! Raus!* Out! Out!" accompanied by gunshots. He grabbed the clogs that he was given when he arrived at the camp – by this point his shoes were already gone – and ran out to the *Appelplatz*. Standing there, flanked by numerous SS men, was an enormously tall officer. Salek judged him to be almost seven feet tall. Major Dalski[5] was wearing high boots and an exquisitely tailored uniform. His large, wolflike dog, whom he addressed as Mensch, circled around him. He referred to the Jews as "dogs."

The inmates stood before him as he screamed with the voice of a madman, "*Hör mal gut zu! Ihr habt die Möglichkeit nach Palästina zu fahren. Ich glaube, wenn jemand nach Palästina fahren möchte*

5. According to rumor, just before the conclusion of the war, Dalski, and the fortune that he had plundered, found a safe haven in Switzerland.

kann er fahren. Die anderen, welche hier arbeiten mochten, können bleiben. Listen to me carefully. I have the opportunity to send you to Palestine. I believe, if somebody wants to travel to Palestine, he can travel. The other way, the other ones can stay here and work."

It made no sense at all. Dalski was offering anybody who wished the chance to leave for Palestine. "Whoever wants to go to Palestine," he ordered, "raise your hand."

The prisoners stood there in total stupefaction until they saw that there was no correlation between the request and what was granted. He ignored those whose hands were raised if they weren't feeble. The strong workers were obviously still needed in the factories.

There were roughly four hundred people in the *Appelplatz*. Those who had been selected for *Palästina* were ordered to return to their barracks and collect their belongings. The remainder were not allowed to move.

It was November 1942, and since he had arrived in June, Salek had learned never to volunteer for anything. In this case, whether you raised your hand or not was irrelevant anyway. Dalski employed the same technique as Skladowski, approaching from behind. Over a hundred people were selected and left the formation.

The ill-fated morning should have been an omen for what would happen later that day. The night shift was unbearable. Everything went wrong, including the generator breaking down and the manual backup malfunctioning. It was a test of ultimate endurance to hold out until morning when it would all be over. Just as the prisoners were settling into some much-deserved sleep, Skladowski burst in swearing like a maniac that the roads must be cleared.

Because of Skladowski's emergency orders, everyone missed their bread and coffee that day. Indeed, Salek was the only one who received anything to eat, thanks, as always, to Helena, the *Lagerführerin* who had free access to food. She would call Salek by name and instruct him to wash her soup container. Unbeknownst to anyone else, the container was never empty, and this way she kept the boy alive.

Out in the streets and fields the prisoners found heaps of shoes, underwear, caps, eyeglasses – anything that a man or woman might wear. Everyone was perplexed by the strange assortment and the huge bloodstains everywhere. The innocent Jews, reared on kindness and benevolence, could not make heads or tails of the sight.

After the prisoners had gathered the loot, they were forced to haul it to a warehouse. There they were ordered to open up the hems of clothing and remove the heels of the shoes to verify that nothing of value had been concealed. Following this they were to sort the garments.

Schmidt was the officer in charge of the sorting, and his orders were very explicit: every piece of metal on one side, diamonds, jewelry, gold, silver, teeth, etc., on the other. Clothing was to be folded and piled in yet a different location. Anyone who deviated in the slightest would be shot. He held his pistol aloft, aching to demonstrate his point.

Despite all of the feverish sorting there was hardly anything of value, aside from a few rings and chains. The clothing was so saturated with blood that it got in the eyes and hair of the prisoners and stained everything. Schmidt was very disappointed by the haul, and when his own inspection yielded a concealed item he went mad, savagely beating people.

Polish machine-operators from nearby villages who had been employed by the Polish government before the war would come to the camp to instruct the Jews on how to work the machinery. When they arrived at the factory that day, they revealed what the naive Jewish inmates could not fathom.

"We saw Jews forced to undress and then loaded onto cattle cars." Different rumors and theories circulated, but the unanimous conclusion was that Treblinka, not Palestine, was the final destination.

Upon hearing this Salek resolved once again that, no matter what, he was going to escape. This desire, shared by countless Jews trapped in Europe, was understandable but sophomoric. Even if the escape would be successful, and even if an untold number of Jews would not have to pay a collective price for one Jew's flight, to where, precisely, was one to escape? There was no way to blend in, for the tattered clothing was a mark of Cain – identifying a Jewish escapee. The Poles were bound to report any Jew seeking shelter if they didn't do away with him themselves.

One evening, the inmates were witness to yet another tragically comical scene. Herring broke into the compound having an infantile fit. Where were his trained specialists, the backbone of his workforce?

Due to Nazi incompetence they had been chosen for Palestine! They were more dead than alive, denied food, sanitation, and sleep – yet they were trained!

One day the SS announced that the whole camp was being transferred. Everyone was ordered to undress, rinse themselves, and deposit their "clothing" with the *werkschutz*. Salek had a coat that was sent by Apt's *Judenrat* and actually got through, but he was forced to leave it in the pile. Even the prisoners' mouths were inspected to verify that nothing was being concealed.

The next stop on the way out of the Skarzysko-Kamienna labor camp was a room where new clothing was waiting for the inmates. They all dressed in the dark blue trousers, thin and poorly made striped shirts, and crude clogs. There was no underwear.

Everyone assumed that they were now ready to depart. Alas, Nazi guile had outsmarted them again. The prisoners had amassed, salvaged, and received a number of odds and ends since their capture, but now these were gone for good. The whole "transfer" was a ruse to despoil the prisoners of everything that they owned.

The inmates were marched back to their old barracks as their masters got the satisfaction of knowing that the only way they could get the Jews to take all of their precious items was by duping them into believing that they were leaving.

Bereft of watches, calendars, and any information connecting them with the world outside, Salek relied on the fact that he heard carols being sung to conclude that it was Christmas. As he and the other Jews desperately clung onto life amid the squalor and torturous conditions, the SS celebrated a religious holiday with wine, women, laughter, and song.

***

One day the factory's generator broke down yet again, crippling the entire factory and sending Herring into a fuming rage. Someone was going to have to pay the price for his anger, and he left nothing to the imagination. Four boys, Salek among them, were selected and Stein, one of the other department heads, joined the festivities. None of these boys had anything to do with the generator breaking down and the work being brought to a standstill.

Herring, armed with a rubber-covered steel rod with a protruding insignia, called over his first victim. "*Bist du Jude?* Are you Jewish?"

He said he was.

"*Bist du religiös?* Are you religious?"

He didn't know what to say. What could he say? He answered, "No."

"*Was? Ein Jude und nicht religiös?* What? You are Jewish, but not religious?" Bang! He beat him across the face and the insignia ripped open the boy's skin. Blood streamed down.

"*Was ist der Beruf deines Vaters?* What is your father's livelihood?"

Each of the boys was asked a similar question. They answered honestly: tailor, shoemaker, and the like.

"*Oh, das glaube ich nicht, er war ein Bankier!* Oh, I don't believe you, he must have been a banker!" Bang, swat! Each line triggered another furious swipe across the face, tearing a deep gash and emitting a river of blood.

"*Du lügst!*" he insisted. "You are lying!"

"*Hast Du die Warheit gesagt?* Did you speak the truth?" He answered yes, he had told the truth.

"*Was? Ein Jude der die Warheit gesagt hat?* What? You are Jewish and you told the truth?!"

Bang, bang, bang. Blood streamed everywhere. Next boy, more questions.

"*Bist du intelligent?* Are you intelligent?" He said he thought so.

"*Was? Ein Jude und intelligent?* What? You are Jewish and intelligent?"

The merciless beatings continued unabated. Herring was assisted by other Nazi officers, who also had some of their own snide questions to pose. Two German women seated by the side of the room crossed their legs and laughed in amusement. With the ultimate politesse, Herring inquired whether the ladies were enjoying the entertainment.

The sadist then turned to his next victim and asked, "*Bist du ein Jude?* Are you Jewish?"

"Yes."

"*Du musst mir das zeigen.* You must show me."

The boy dropped his trousers and Herring took the opportunity to invite the women to cross the room and have a good look.

Herring then approached Salek, looked up at the clock and said, "*Ich glaube die Maschinen haben angefangen zu arbeiten.* I believe that the machines have started working again," almost forgetting to beat him. But "almost" for Torture-über-*alles*-Herring did not exist. He reverted to type and justified the torture: "*Ohne nichts koennen wir ihn nicht gehen lassen.* I cannot allow him to proceed without any punishment." He rattled off pointless, rhetorical questions prior to whipping Salek's legs, leaving gashes, welts, and other bruises that would never fade.

For the *coup de grace,* Herring inspected his prey to determine how many blows the boys should receive before being dismissed. The final lashing was to atone for answers that had not pleased him. No answers could – but this could not absolve them from punishment. The boys were ordered to remove their clothing for the Jewish overseers to whip them.

The victims had to count each lash out loud. The pain was so intense that it was almost impossible to breathe, but the boys nonetheless counted, aware that the alternative would have been even worse. *Eins, zwei, drei, vier, fünf.* If a boy erred in his counting, or if he fainted in the middle, he would have to start again from the beginning.

Although Herring claimed that he was in a rush, he had all the time in the world to interrupt the counting, feign that he did not hear correctly, or manufacture whatever excuse he fancied to restart the nearly finished counting. And as Herring guffawed, the bodies of the boys turned black from congealed blood under their skin.

When Herring had had his fill, the proceedings were curtailed. Salek could no longer walk – he could barely crawl – yet he had to be back at work at three o'clock in the morning. The worst, everyone understood, was still to come. The generator was bound to break down again and the whole torturous spectacle would be repeated, rendering four more boys cripples for life for the amusement of the ladies and sadistic Herring.

Of course the SS did not need the pretext of a broken generator to perpetrate their torture. One of Salek's friends, Dundela, was hauled into the camp office and ordered to sing his favorite song. His performance did not adequately please the assembled company, leading to a beating which left him staggering back to the barracks, like the four Herring victims, completely battered.

The suffering inflicted gave Salek a new perspective: Dalski and his false promise of *Palästina* didn't sound so bad after all. At least he had sent them to their deaths and to rest in peace. This was denied to the living.

***

Not long after these torture sessions, everyone was summoned to the *Appelplatz*. This did not augur well. The camp's commanding officer ranted and raved until the assembled understood that two Jews from Stopnic, a little town not far from Apt, had escaped. Salek knew them both.

The two had done the unthinkable and it warranted Nazi justice. The terrified prisoners held their breath as the verdict was decreed: for each missing prisoner ten others were to be executed. Slowly and deliberately, the SS made their selection, pulling out twenty feeble individuals on the verge of collapse. One of them was Salek.

Helena, the *Lagerführerin* and Salek's guardian angel, watched the scene unfold and committed a daring act of intervention. "No, not this one!" she insisted. "He has nothing to do with the escapees! Put him back!" On Helena's say-so, Salek was returned to "the living."

Next to Salek stood a boy not more than thirteen or fourteen years old. He had arrived from one of the ghettos and had been in the camp for less than a month. He was so new, in fact, that he still wore a neat, blue wool jacket fastened with a buckle, brought from home. It was apparent that this boy had come from an affluent family.

Guilty of no crime other than being Jewish and standing next to a formerly condemned victim, the boy was ordered to remove his jacket and hand it Salek. He was then marched off to his execution as Salek put on the martyr's mantle.

It wasn't until the survivors were back in their barracks that they heard a volley of shots followed by deathly silence. The *Totengeneral* later related that before the boys were murdered they were forced to dig their own graves. But as the ground was frozen, the most that they could do was scratch out a shallow groove. They didn't even merit a burial.

Salek hardly reveled in the sudden reversal of his death sentence that had taken everyone by surprise. Even before he was condemned to death he had been looking forward to being reunited with his family after death, and this opportunity had been cruelly snatched from him. Furthermore, he was haunted by the memory of the little boy who was sent to death in his place.

Day after day Salek could not fall asleep. He agonized over the twenty victims who were shot because of the two escapees and the fact that he was, in a sense, responsible for the death of the boy with the blue jacket.

Once again Helena came to the rescue by consoling him. "Orenstein," she said, "you've got to remember that they were choosing people from the same town as the escapees. You did not live there. You don't have to torture yourself!" At last these words provided a modicum of comfort to Salek, although he never forgot the young boy, whose name he never knew.

Chapter Eight

Chance Meeting: My Yellow Brother!

Lice were a constant torment for the prisoners of Skarzysko and indeed, for any prisoner under Nazi dominion. Black bugs, normally tiny specks, grew to fist-sized, behemoth proportions, having fed on an endless supply of Jewish blood. There were different varieties, but what they all had in common was a tenacious determination to bleed the victim white. They would embed themselves so deep that brushing, shaking, and even scraping could not dislodge them. Only a determined incision into the skin with a sharp thumbnail might do the trick. But such a painful procedure could eliminate only one at a time, and there were hundreds!

Because Salek's skin was coated with the malodorous machine oil he was less appetizing to the lice than the others. Unfortunately, not all varieties of lice are fussy. His "relatively" better situation still rendered him a walking bug colony. His blanket (much too grand a description for something that was nothing more than a threadbare *shmatteh*), which he had purloined from somewhere around the factory, was thoroughly infested with lice.

The blanket stayed with Salek at all times. When he wasn't sleeping he would wrap it around himself and tuck it under his clothing. If it wasn't actually on his body there was no doubt that such a valuable commodity – a threadbare, smelly, lice-infested, coarse cloth – would disappear.

Across the yard from the factory there was a small fire that was always burning. Each time he went to the latrine, Salek would make sure to pass by the fire and surreptitiously hold his blanket up to the flames. The heat would dislodge a good number of lice, and they produced a crackling sound when they hit the fire. Naturally the fire would singe the blanket and other lice would take the place of their dead comrades, but it was good to know that an effort was being made to contain the menace and that he was not being complacent about his lot.

Every once in a while the workers in the factory were deloused. The point of the disinfection was in no way to provide a service to the expendable Jewish slave force. It was done strictly to protect the Nazis, who feared infection by the lice that plagued the workers. Of course if a German were to contract typhus, the dreaded disease that was spread by the lice, he would be hospitalized and receive medical care. A Jew with typhus was no longer an asset to the workforce and was shot. Accordingly, a Jew in Skarzysko rarely died a natural death.

The disinfection did not come soon enough for Salek. He came down with dreaded typhus, resulting in a soaring temperature. He was possessed by hallucinations and was deemed insane by his barrack mates. Salek had a dream where he saw his parents arriving by horse and wagon to bring him back to a homecoming party. Everyone was there, clapping their hands for their hero, hugging and kissing him, even Salek's grandfather, "Zeide," who had died four years earlier.

As vivid and realistic as the dream was, he soon woke to the same squalor of the barrack, dangerously ill. A doctor stopped by and determined that he was at the worst stage, somewhere between the twelfth and fourteenth day. Helena, the *Lagerführerin* and Salek's constant savior, saw to it that he received some water. But the greatest salvation came from Above.

During this period, when Salek was not an asset to the Third Reich and hence a candidate for elimination, *Werk* B, where he was assigned, was relocated to *Werk* A. During the period of transition the machinery was dismantled and production was suspended. Therefore Salek was not absent for a single day of work and in the chaos of the move he was not even missed. Salek's luck – and the only reason he survived the illness undetected – was all due to the timing. Chaos was his salvation.

There were no washing facilities in *Werk* B. But in *Werk* A, where they were moved that summer, there was a *paruvke,* a building with an anteroom where you deposited your clothing for delousing and a large shower hall with moderately warm water.

The opportunity to wash was cause for celebration for those who had been deprived for so long. For the filthy, grimy victims of the Holocaust it took only a few drops of water to cause jubilation. But this cause for rejoicing paled in comparison to what Salek saw next...

Awaiting his turn to bathe, a boy approached him, saying, "Salek? Is that you?" At first he was sure it was an apparition, a hallucination from his typhus-riddled brain. But this time he was not delirious, and indeed, right in front of him was Yehuda Fischel, his older brother!

Salek had had no idea that he had been there in the camp; he didn't even know that he was alive. Yehuda Fischel recognized his younger brother, but Salek had trouble believing it was him.

Salek's failure to recognize his brother was hardly just a result of trauma and deprivation. It took a while for Salek to be convinced that Yehuda Fischel was actually his brother because the boy was bright yellow!

Yehuda Fischel explained that he was working in *Werk* C, where he and the other "yellows" produced the internal contents of the artillery shells. It was unbelievable, like a specter from a science fiction novel, until Salek saw other workers from the same division looking like a bunch of bananas in tattered prison garb. Still others were green.

The "yellows" worked in Picric and the "greens" worked in Trottil. The "yellows" had it better than the "greens," who worked in a highly toxic environment. Yehuda Fischel explained that the appalling and lethal coloring did not exist prior to the war.

Before the Nazi invasion, all those who worked in the toxic environment of the weapons factory were provided with appropriate protective clothing and masks. Health and safety issues were addressed, and it was unthinkable to expose a worker to chemicals that would painfully disfigure and kill him.

That was prior to the war. Now, none of the most ghastly colored prisoners survived more than a few weeks.

In their few fleeting moments together the brothers exchanged as much information as was possible. Yehuda Fischel believed that their older sister, Pola, was still alive. This belief was based on the fact that the two of them had managed to escape and hide with a Polish farmer after his parents were deported from Apt to Treblinka. The farmer had reluctantly agreed to hide Pola in his hayloft in exchange for her grandmother's textiles, which had been cleverly hidden away for safekeeping. Pola worked for him attired in Polish peasant clothing.

The encounter culminated with Yehuda Fischel giving Salek a slice of bread. The treasure was acquired dearly. Yehuda Fischel had informed a non-Jew in the factory about his father's business connection in the country where he had left money and goods. All of the Orenstein possessions were redeemed for one slice of bread.

"Something is better than nothing," Yehuda Fischel consoled him wryly, as he gave away the full barter of his family's assets.

Leaving the washhouse, Salek noticed that one boy was standing slightly out of line. He was clearly having difficulty walking. Salek had slept next to this boy and had grown quite close to him. The *werkschutz* began to shout, and from the way that he was gesticulating, Salek thought that the enraged Ukrainian guard was yelling at him. The confusion was settled when the *werkschutz* shot Salek's friend for deviating from the formation. He then gave the victim a good kicking to make sure that he was really dead. Salek would never be able to shake the memory of his final image of that boy, his hands raised in front of his face, futilely attempting to shield himself.

When Salek was relocated to *Werk* A he was careful to suppress his knowledge of how to operate a lead machine. He was thus spared that messy labor in favor of a far easier job at an extrusion machine, where he became an expert. Overall, *Werk* A was an improvement over *Werk* B, especially as each machine was fitted with its own motor and not hooked up to a central generator.

These improvements, however, did little to arrest the appalling death rate. Due to continuous selections, each day there were fewer workers. The weak and seriously debilitated were sent away to the death camps, and remnants from the almost-defunct ghettos trickled in to replace them.

Werk A also had a few new officers, including a bespectacled man named Bosch, who gave the impression of being a true academic. Bosch lacked the level of cruelty so prevalent among the others, and his interest was production, not torture.

When he heard how Herring had abused the workers and interfered with production, Bosch scolded, "If you don't behave yourself, I'll send you to the eastern front!"

Bosch noticed Salek's proficiency with his machine and promoted him to being a supervisor responsible for three other machines. This was in 1944, when Salek had been at the Hassag work camp in Skarzysko for over three years.

***

There was a Jewish girl from Krakow together with Salek, whose beauty could not be diminished by the terrible conditions at Skarzysko. She had mesmerizing blue eyes, curly, fair hair, and delicate features. Salek saw something extraordinary about this girl. She was from Krakow and told him about her life in the ghetto. He was very attracted to her and said to himself, "It scarcely seems possible, but I must admit that I have fallen in love with her." Accordingly, he summoned up all of his courage and made an advance.

Under the circumstances, Salek could not have looked better. He was wearing the (freshly deloused) little blue jacket with the buckle that he had inherited from the martyr who had taken his place. As a matter of fact, by Salek's slave-labor–tempered standards, he was dashing!

Salek discovered that she was beautiful inside as well. Rochel described to him her life in the ghetto. A man had lost his wife and was left alone with his young daughter. He found it difficult to take care of her. Rochel, on a voluntary basis, tended to the little girl the entire time she lived in the ghetto. Salek concluded that if it was possible to be noble in the bowels of the Holocaust, then it was also possible to fall in love.

Such was the fantasia of the Holocaust, when one did not know with certainty if one would live out the day; one could dream of marrying a woman when it was unlikely he would ever see her again.

Because of overlapping shifts the couple met often. Rochel reminded Salek of his younger sister and he felt very protective toward her. They conversed in Polish since Rochel did not understand Yiddish.

Salek wished to give Rochel something tangible as proof of their friendship. This was an enormous challenge because he had nothing to call his own. When an opportunity finally presented itself, Salek leapt at it. He approached Rochel and offered her a portion of bread that he had left over from Yehuda Fischel. He carefully broke the piece into two and held out half to her. Shyly, she refused, although she was clearly tempted. "Your brother gave it to you," she said with conviction. "It's for you."

***

One morning Salek slept right through the emergency wake-up call announced over the loudspeaker. The crack of gunfire, however, did succeed in waking him. The barrack was deserted. Salek remained on his slat, pressed against the side of the wall, utterly still and taking up no space. The Jewish overseers who rushed in to verify that the barracks were empty did not notice him.

For about an hour Salek lay totally still, barely breathing. Finally, the prisoners shuffled back to the barracks, silent as death. The man who slept below Salek was kind and mature, a father figure who often spoke longingly of his wife and family. Normally the man had a very pleasant demeanor, but that morning he was horribly downcast.

He looked up at Salek and commented softly, "You were lucky to have missed what we just saw. We were forced to witness the hanging of eight boys: the two who had escaped from Treblinka and an additional six." It was these two boys who had escaped from Treblinka who informed Salek about when his parents were murdered. In Treblinka, like most of the other extermination camps, the day the prisoners arrived was the day they were gassed.

A different boy in the barrack added that the boys were actually smiling as they stepped up to the gallows. In moments they would finally be freed from Skarzysko and transported to a world that could only be better. "One noose broke," the barrack mate continued, "and the boy had to be hanged again."

When Salek left for his shift the bodies were still dangling and he recognized their faces. This was yet another image that was all but impossible to erase.

Chapter Nine

Tortured Beyond Human Endurance

In April of 1944, Polish workers related that the Russian army was on the march. As ignorance among the prisoners was absolute, no one knew if this boded well or not. This report was followed by a flurry of rumors that the Germans were going to liquidate all of the workers. Conditions seemed to deteriorate and the psychological stress was ratcheted up, turning uncertainty into exquisite agony.

As rumors continued to fly, the Germans announced that the factory was going to be moved to another site fifty miles away. Despite the workers' keen awareness of the German talent to mislead and dupe, this still sounded a tad encouraging.

That night the prisoners were divided into groups and led to the railway tracks. No one knew what the final destination would be, although most assumed that the choices were either Schweiden or Auschwitz. Schweiden was a different munitions factory and the function of Auschwitz at this point in the war was well known (except to the Allied governments, who feigned ignorance until the end …).

There were probably five hundred prisoners standing at the railway tracks waiting when a small locomotive with open wagons finally arrived. The SS got to work loading their cargo as dogs howled and strained on their leashes, aching to tear the prisoners apart.

Bosch arrived and issued strict instructions that his workforce was to be taken to Schenlechau and under no circumstances was the train to be diverted anywhere else. There was no love lost between Bosch and the Jewish people, but he had a job to do and *they* were going to do it!

At least a hundred people were crammed so tightly into each wagon that it was impossible to sit down. The journey took a full three days and throughout, death was everywhere. There was no option other than to stand on the deceased, and even after all that he had seen, Salek had never witnessed such horrid scenes of death.

His prize possession, two little containers he had found in the factory and filled with water, kept him going – barely – for the duration of the trip. The youngest prisoners, who had survived until then on miniscule portions of soup, bread, and black water, were proving the most resilient. Those between the ages of thirteen and twenty-three seemed to have the best chance; they were pliable like young saplings and able to weather the devastating storm. The older ones simply snapped.

It was at this point that the Russian army's advance ground to a halt at the eastern bank of the Vistula River. Had they only continued the offensive the prisoners would have been liberated, but Stalin had his own agenda. Washington and London were pressing for the offensive to continue. Stalin, however, saw a long-term gain for the Russian empire if the Poles liberated themselves. Thus, at that critical juncture when the death camps were still operational, the Russians dug in just three miles from Auschwitz. Tens of thousands of Jews could have been saved from the death march, from which a scant ten percent of prisoners survived, but human life – particularly Jewish life – was never a consideration for Stalin.

All of the rumors and tangible hopes of liberation were quashed due to the machinations of political leaders.

When the train arrived at Transilow in the summer of 1944 the prisoners were eager to get off as quickly as possible. After being sealed in amid corpses, waste, and vomit for several days, however, no one was physically or mentally able to jump down. This, of course, was of little concern to the Germans, who ordered the stronger ones to toss off the weaker ones.

The prisoners had never heard of Transilow, which was one of the main ammunition centers for the German army.

Initiation rites in a new camp were always hellish from the very first lineup. The arrivals were ordered to leave everything on the ground even though they weren't carrying anything. The rapacious Germans always assumed that Jews were carrying gold, silver, or precious jewelry. They commanded anyone with a weapon to raise his hand, which was ridiculous; had anyone raised a hand he would have been shot.

The only nourishment provided was some black water that was dispensed at midnight. Following this the Jewish overseers directed the arrivals into two empty barracks free of the standard straw and rags that were inevitably infested with lice.

That night presented a tremendous test of endurance since it was impossible to lie down. There wasn't even enough room to sit. There were only three beds, and those who foolishly attempted to take advantage of them were stepped on and crushed.

After the morning roll call the arrivals were ordered to report to the machines that they had worked on previously so that the "masters" could select slaves for their departments. Salek lined up at the extrusion machine at which he was competent.

Selections were made and then the workers were marched into factories that barely differed from the ones where they had worked before. Still, the new factory was more modern and better equipped, and the supervision was less draconian. The *werkschutz* at Transilow were not as trigger-happy as their comrades in Skarzysko, nor were they as curious to see how sharp their bayonets were.

The Skarzysko arrivals were in such a debilitated state that the veterans at the camp were appalled by their condition. Among the astounded was Zeifman, a former neighbor of the Orensteins from Apt. How she was able to recognize Salek was beyond him, for he could not have weighed more than forty-five pounds.

Zeifman had some influence in the camp and she negotiated some bread and soup for him. As in the past, Salek fantasized about escaping, but Zeifman was quick to pour cold water on his plan. "You think it's so easy?" she said. "Where will you go? It's obvious where you're from!"

She also introduced Salek to the famous author Nachum Perlman, but the young Orenstein was not familiar with this literary giant. Perlman latched onto Salek at once, as he knew his family and wished to be of assistance. Salek, however, was unable to pay attention to Perlman's endless list of achievements or discuss his erudite books. Typhoid fever had seriously affected his hearing, rendering him all but deaf. None of this stopped Perlman, who endlessly regaled his newfound audience.

The author conspiratorially informed Salek about a top-secret meeting that would soon take place. Revealing anything about it would cost Salek his life. At that meeting Salek was introduced to Godzia, a young woman from Apt who was about the same age as his older sister. Godzia easily diagnosed Salek's deafness as typhus-related, and shouted and gestured to convey her message.

With a piece of wire she sewed a fifty-dollar note into the hem of his trousers and explained that if the opportunity would present itself to jump off an Auschwitz-bound train this money might prove lifesaving. In addition, she gave him a hard, dry biscuit which she had managed to acquire from a Pole. It was preferable to bread as it would last longer. If he nibbled on it sparingly, it might sustain him long enough to find a safe haven. The biscuit was as black as soot, but it was pure manna and Salek guarded it with his life.

***

As autumn turned into winter, a perceptible change could be felt at the camp. The Germans were far more concerned about their own future than afflicting their Jewish charges. They suspected that the Russians would renew their offensive in the winter when they had a natural advantage over the cold-fearing Germans.

One day the prisoners were driven out of the barracks to wait outside during a fierce snowstorm. For hours they stood at attention as the snow swirled around them and chilled their bones. Finally, a delegation of the SS, including soldiers from the regular German army, arrived, their winter helmets pulled down snugly.

When the command was issued, the SS, holding back wolflike dogs straining at the leash, divided the camp into hundreds and herded them onto a waiting train. This was no simple maneuver. The prisoners were stiff and nearly frozen to death. Alas, the Nazis had their methods to get anyone to move, and at double time!

The doors of the train were closed and nailed shut with six-inch nails that penetrated the walls. It would still be hours before the train would depart and three full days without food or drink before the doors would be opened. Men who had survived the abuse of Dalski and Herring never thought they would survive this ride. The agony was unbearable, and many went insane. The only thing that kept them quiet was the fact that they were frozen.

Salek happened to have his ration from the day before but could not bring himself to eat it. After two days without food, hunger was insignificant next to the overwhelming thirst that crazed the mind and racked the body.

There were a number who cried out *Shema Yisrael,* certain that they were about to die. But the *musselmanner,* those that the Holocaust had rendered more dead than alive, hardly seemed fazed by the protracted starvation. The *musselmanner,* with Salek teetering on swelling the ranks of this faceless mass of ghosts, had become detached from the world and the ways of humanity. It was quite remarkable that he had not joined them until then. He had lost his family, his clothing, his self-respect, his ability to maintain personal hygiene and even to relieve himself. The one thing he hadn't lost was his will to live.

For the frozen matchsticks, the only emotion that remained was the raging desire to avenge themselves upon the *werkschutz.* But it was a dream never to be realized. The prisoners had given up all hope. Regarding those who later questioned, "Why didn't you resist? The *malech ha'movess* could have come and pushed us over into *Gehinom* with no resistance at all." Some said afterward, "Why didn't you resist? Ask this pencil to resist! It has more life in it than we had! You know why? Because it has a little point! As for us, we were totally useless, worn down."

Chapter Ten

Buchenwald Concentration Camp

Traveling in the dead of winter, the countryside was smothered in a thick blanket of snow. Salek could not tell or even imagine where they were. It might have been heaven; it might have been hell. These were the woods of Buchenwald, nourished with human fertilizer. The Thuringian forests of the region were densely planted with pine trees whose form could barely be discerned under layers of snow.

The prisoners could see nothing but white, empty space. The only noise was the chugging of the locomotive and the occasional blast of the horn.

They were unloaded in front of a pair of huge gates that appeared to be at least fifty feet high. The gates opened and the Jews were marched until they reached two brick sentry boxes at the formal entrance of the Buchenwald concentration camp. The majority of the camp was constructed by communists and mentally challenged individuals who were incarcerated during the 1930s. The first thing Salek noticed in Buchenwald was the seeming absence of the Ukrainian *werkschutz.*

Salek was sent into a cubicle where his name, age, and hometown were recorded. None other than Leon Blum, the former prime minister of France, registered Salek's details. Blum, attempting to spare the lad, insisted that Salek was not a Jew, and gave him a triangle to wear on his sleeve instead of a star, identifying him as a political prisoner.

It was difficult for Salek to respond to the questioning as he was deaf as a post. He therefore carefully watched what was going on and attempted to conceal his disability. Salek was assigned to a barrack, but as he couldn't hear the number he just followed the others and tried to fit in.

Before the new prisoners could enter the barrack, the previous occupants, now deceased, had to be removed. Two inmates stacked up the bodies outside the door like logs, four across, four down so that the pile would not topple over. By this point in the war stacking bodies like cards was neither new nor shocking to Salek. Still, the stench inside the barrack was absolutely dreadful. The corpses had marinated in their own vomit and excrement for some time. This was Salek's new home, one he would share with hundreds of other youngsters, including Elie Wiesel.

The next stop was the delousing room where the prisoners were forced to hand in their clothing. Salek was careful to remove his fifty-dollar bill and clutch it in the palm of his hand. The entrance to the delousing room was one-way only. The cold, hungry new arrivals were shunted down a very narrow, winding staircase that led to a large disinfectant-filled tub that was four feet deep and the size of a dining table.

They were commanded to jump in and submerge their bodies. Six orderlies gripping long sticks saw to it that every inch of their bodies was covered by the chemical potion. Somehow, throughout the entire procedure, Salek held onto his fifty-dollar bill, though his body was on fire.

The orderlies repeatedly jabbed their sticks, and it was clearly immaterial if anyone drowned in the disinfectant. Buchenwald sought a typhus-free environment, and this meant aggressive, often fatal, disinfection.

Salek's eyelids, ears, indeed every part of his skin, was burning from the chemicals. Yet, there was a modicum of consolation for those whose brains were still able to function after being cured in disinfectant. What sense would it make to gas victims after having already wasted chemicals on delousing them?

Following disinfection, the arrivals were shunted into another large room. Instinctively, Salek looked up, as he always did, to see if there were gas vents. All previous theories about the inefficiency of gassing after investing in sanitizing were dispelled as soon as the protrusions from the ceiling were spotted. No one assumed that the shower heads were innocent. Salek thought to himself, "It won't take long."

Gassing had been the main topic of discussion among the Jewish prisoners ever since its implementation became known. All were certain that their next breath of air would be their last.

There were about fifty people in the stall when water, not poisonous gas, poured down. It was the middle of winter and temperatures were subzero, rendering the water freezing. The torturously cold water created ecstasy in the stall. It had been so long since Salek had felt the thrill of water on his back that it generated, unbelievably, a pleasant sensation. Perhaps, Salek contemplated, their bodies were so tense with deathly fear that the effect of the water was relaxing, causing warmth.

From the freezing shower the prisoners were forced into a tub of disinfectant powder that was neither abrasive nor coarse. The feeling was heavenly, and for once Salek's body was free from the lice and parasites that had riddled and punctured his skin.

Naturally, the prisoners were not given towels and were ordered to stand in an area where they drained off prior to being issued their Buchenwald uniforms. Salek noticed that he was standing on a tiled floor. It was the first time in his life he had seen tiles.

The uniform consisted of trousers, a blue and white striped jacket, clogs, a cap, and no undergarments. The uniform was made of real cloth – not the paper-thin covering that they had worn in the other camps. He could tell that it had been mended and only God knew how many prisoners it had survived.

Salek's cap was far too large for him, so he ripped the back of it and tied the ends together in a knot. This made him very easily recognizable, for no one else had a knot in their cap.

Salek was curious about a long screen from behind which came blood-curdling screams. He was hardly prepared for the answer he received. Behind the screen sat a tribunal of three judges. Every Jew who was appointed to a position of power had to prove before the tribunal that he had not abused that post.

There were a vast number of Jewish intellectuals in Buchenwald and they saw to it that the trials were fair and not superficial. Witnesses were called and cross-examinations conducted. Every Jewish policeman was subject to their interrogations and they had to defend themselves by proving that they had not taken advantage of their fellow man or abused the system.

One of the defendants was a short Jewish *kapo* whom Salek could not forget. He was in charge of the prisoners in *Werk* B in Skarzysco and was as cruel as the Ukrainian *werkschutz*. If anyone was out of line by so much as one inch he would beat him mercilessly. It also seemed that he was a misogynist, as he was particularly mean to women. Witnesses from Salek's transport who had suffered from his excesses were called to the stand.

The testimony was damning. They claimed that he sent many "to selection" and had workers removed from machines prematurely; had he left them at their posts a little longer it might have saved their lives. The defendant was condemned to death and was handed a rope and given half an hour to hang himself. If he did not comply, his death would be more gruesome.

Salek related to the tribunal his experiences in Skarzysko and inquired about the fate of Rochel. Would she also be deported or would she remain behind in the labor camp?

Just one month earlier she had related to Salek that the *kapos* were asked to supply six girls from the barracks for a party, and these girls never returned. Everyone assumed that they were raped, as the next day there was an announcement that six girls had tried to escape but were caught and executed.

Rochel was terribly afraid that she would suffer the same fate. No one expected to survive, but to die being violated by those murderers was far worse than the gas chambers.

Chapter Eleven

Spring 1945 – Allied Bombers

After two days at Buchenwald, Salek's group was given assignments, and many were sent to a munitions factory in Schlieben. Salek learned that Yehuda Fischel had also been working there and was killed during an Allied bombing. This news was devastating to Salek.

Otherwise, life in Buchenwald was markedly superior to everywhere else he had been in the Holocaust Kingdom. The constant cruelty and fear of death that hovered over the prisoners in the slave-labor camps was hardly as dominating in the concentration camp. The SS, with their terrifying skull and crossbones insignia and black leather coats, were only nominally involved in the daily running of the camp. Rather, the political prisoners, who wore a different uniform than the other prisoners, were in charge.

The stout political prisoner in charge of Salek was a nice man. His interest, like that of the camp directorate, was that orders be obeyed. They were not looking for infractions so that they could punish and torture. The distribution of food was also much fairer than what Salek was accustomed to. The political prisoners saw to it that everyone received an equal share and that there was no cheating. They even made sure that the soup was well mixed so that its contents would be evenly distributed.

Still, the conditions in Buchenwald were highly conducive to death from starvation, exposure, disease, or injury. However, it was primarily a sadism-free environment. Salek maintained that the different types of people with whom he came into contact in Buchenwald, from so many different races and religions, ultimately made him a better person equipped to appreciate every human being.

Salek was already sixteen but looked much younger, so he was moved from barrack 66 to barrack 54. Opposite the *kinderlager*, separated by a wire fence, was the women's compound. One of the barracks there was devoted to serving the vices of the German officers. Young women sat in front on display. All day long soldiers entered and exited, adjusting their clothing on their way out.

Henry, a non-Jewish Slav from Lidice, slept next to Salek. He tried every which way to befriend Salek and engage in conversation, which was quite a feat considering Salek's state of near-deafness. Henry made a point of standing next to Salek during the *appel* and would call out his number at the right time, saving Salek's life on many occasions.

One day during work, a group of prisoners, Salek included, was taken to the nearby bombed-out town of Weimar, which needed to have its rubble cleared.

The excavation work yielded all kinds of objects, including bodies. Most importantly, food was discovered among the debris. No one knew if the food was poisoned or not, but for hunger-crazed men that was all but irrelevant.

The results were immediate. The extra calories consumed in those three days of rubble-clearing produced immediate results, transforming the emaciated men into a faint reflection of their former robust selves. Even what wasn't noticeable to the eye was very apparent in the recovery of strength that they all felt.

Clearing out the wreckage, Salek hoisted an overturned cupboard, and a pile of linen and shirts fell out. He helped himself to the goods by tying clothing around his waist, shoving some articles down his trouser legs and employing every trick that he could imagine without appearing too conspicuous. Everyone was searched upon returning to the camp, so taking too much booty was not worth the risk.

Every day Salek would smuggle different items from Weimar back to the camp. One day, he discovered several cans of sardines and managed to bring them into the camp undetected. The starving boy found himself in an ironic situation, to say the least. The food was tempting, his hunger was gnawing, but Salek had no way of opening the cans!

Eventually, he found a sharp tool at the factory with which he succeeded in prying open the lid. However, the clumsy tool, coupled with Salek's haste, caused the oil to spill out. He was terribly frustrated at the time, but in hindsight he realized that had such a quantity of fat been ingested by someone as emaciated as Salek, it might have been lethal.

Along with the spoils gathered from the Weimar rubble clearing was the tremendous satisfaction derived from the destruction of German property. The city was largely in ruins, and this spoke volumes about the tide of the war.

The Reich was shrinking. More prisoners were arriving at Buchenwald, a camp that was actually within the official borders of Germany. The only way to accommodate the great influx was to remove the dead and the near-dead. Salek had trouble discerning the live from the dead that were carted away, so feeble was their hold on life.

Many of the newcomers to Buchenwald were Hungarians who had just been deported three or four weeks earlier. Even though their privations were nominal compared with the veterans, the Hungarians could not cope with their plight. They moaned and groaned interminably, crying that they did not want to die.

It was hard for the old-timers to respect those so consumed by self-pity. All night long they spoke about the goulash and meatballs they used to eat in Budapest's finest restaurants. They rattled on and on, playing on the nerves of the senior prisoners. "Can't you shut up!" the veterans would shout, but those formerly prosperous individuals could not be reasoned with.

Far more annoying than this was the problem that Salek, and so many others, suffered from. Their bodies were bereft of any fat to serve as padding and were covered in sores, making it nearly impossible to lie down on their bunks. Salek looked like a tightly fitting sack of bones, which meant that every part of his body was sensitive and sore.

One day, inmates were taken to a long building that they had never seen before. It was an exquisitely designed washroom with a tiled floor and rows and rows of sinks and taps! The prisoners were ordered to scrub the sinks and polish the faucets until they gleamed; nothing less would be acceptable. All of the work was to be done with rags and water in buckets that the prisoners were equipped with. Under no circumstance were they allowed to use the taps.

Salek's sink had some particularly stubborn black stains that he could not dislodge, hard as he tried. In desperation he turned on the tap, but nothing came out! Although the tap did not work, German publicity was hard at work.

Count Bernadotte, a Swedish official, was coming to inspect the camp on behalf of the Red Cross. The Nazis, who had long ago perfected the art of public relations, artifice, and deception, seized the opportunity as only they could. The pristine, clean washhouse, with its neatly folded towels and all of the conventional bathroom accessories, had been prepared exclusively for Bernadotte's visit, but it was never intended – or even designed – to be used!

The real facilities at Buchenwald – not adorned with window dressing – did not even have doors. No paper of any sort was ever provided. It took tremendous stamina and ingenuity to keep oneself clean, and Salek realized that he had no other choice if he wished to live, for the sore skin draped tautly over his skeleton was rotting away.

Apparently Bernadotte struck a deal with the SS, for a few hundred female prisoners were released, either for money or as part of some publicity negotiations, to safe haven in Sweden.

One night, inexplicably, Salek did not report to his night shift. All night long American planes flew above. A Russian Jew in Salek's barrack who had a military background assessed that once the Americans had gathered sufficient reconnaissance information, Buchenwald would be flattened and no one would survive.

Fortunately, he was only partially correct. Bombs fell that night, wiping out the industrial compound. Most of the workers on Salek's shift were killed. The few survivors were forced to salvage machines and scrap metal from the rubble.

The spring of 1945 brought heavy rains. The unpaved paths were converted into fields of mud that were treacherous death traps. Stepping into the mud – which was unavoidable – meant losing your clogs or shoes. The prisoners had no other recourse but to crawl on all fours in order to get to where they needed to go.

Chapter Twelve

The Death Train

One chilly spring day, all the Jews were ordered to leave their barracks. In a moment of insanity Salek complied, even though according to camp records he was not a Jew. They were forced to march outside the camp to a different set of train tracks from the ones that had brought them to Buchenwald. All the while, German soldiers on motorcycles and jeeps rode smugly past the pitiful skeletons.

They marched and marched. Those who could not keep pace with the group were shot and kicked into the ditch. Every few yards there was another casualty. The prisoners walked four abreast, but the longer they marched the smaller the formation became.

After four hours of marching there were more than one hundred moaning casualties lying by the side of the road, blood seeping out of their wasted bodies. Only toward evening did the open, filthy freight cars arrive. The detritus of their previous cargo of rocks, sand, and coal still lined the floors of the carriages.

It was only then that the extent of Salek's lunacy hit him. He could have been back in the camp instead of marching to his death at a railway siding. Even more senseless was the presence of Salek's Slavic friend, Henry, who *really* wasn't a Jew. The boy was definitely a fool!

The prisoners were parched. They had not had a drop to drink since setting out in the morning and were gasping from thirst. Eventually a bucket of water that had been drawn off the steam engine was passed around. In order to get a mouthful the men had to stick their heads into the bucket like animals, but no one refrained.

The prisoners boarded the carriages. After traveling through the night, the train slowed down at daybreak. Mustering their greatest linguistic prowess, the prisoners managed to exchange a few words with French POWs, who were still wearing the tattered remains of their French army uniforms and were working on the tracks. The French found the notion that the Jews were being shipped to work in heavy military industry hilarious.

"What, these skeletons?" they mocked.

A short farmer in a Tyrolean hat arrived, accompanied by the SS. He desperately needed workers, but he would not have Jews contaminate his property. Still, he performed an examination, peering into everyone's ears! Ultimately, he rejected the whole lot, but before he sent them away, he uncharacteristically offered some food. It was a mystery that was compounded when Salek overheard him comment to an SS officer, "They are all filthy Jews – send them *home*!"

A truck arrived bearing several large pots of soup. It had been twenty-four hours since they had left Buchenwald and they were desperately hungry. Although the soup had an odd taste and was extremely salty, the famished prisoners wolfed down the contents of the pots. Salek was so slow that by the time he reached the truck all of the soup was gone. Some old, moldy bread was then tossed onto the train cars but he did not manage to grab a piece of that either, and he was thoroughly dejected.

A river ran close to the track. For those who could manage the distance, it was a chance to lap up some water. Salek also found some nettles to eat. They tasted sweet but their needles stung his tongue. The pain was excruciating and consistently worsened. Over the course of the day Salek's tongue swelled to three times its size and he could not be understood; only gibberish came out of his mouth.

That night, many fell ill, vomiting terribly. Once again Salek had been spared, as the soup and bread had been poisoned. Half of the prisoners on the train expired and in the morning they were loaded onto the *Totenwagen*. The corpses were piled so high that the entire cart was full.

Those in Salek's car deliberately did not remove all of the corpses. They served a utilitarian purpose as benches and were a marked improvement over the filth of the car floor. Eventually, the stench emanating from the corpses became so unbearable that the drawback outweighed the benefit, and the "benches" had to be removed.

Salek devoured any plant, root, or vegetation[6] that he could lay his hands on. One day he discovered half a rotten potato lying on the ground. Normally, who would try to eat an unwashed, rotten potato coated with dirt?

Salek was in no position to be finicky. Little did he realize that the spud would dry out his mouth and make him insane with thirst; it also triggered terrible diarrhea. Sometimes he simply created more problems than he solved.

Eventually, the train reached the German industrial city of Chemnitz. Until then the train had never stopped at a station where the passengers could be observed. At this station plenty of

6. A doctor in Theresienstadt later told him that the vitamins in the vegetation were probably what saved him.

German civilians were milling about and able to observe the pitiful skeletons in the open cars. A high-ranking officer announced over a bullhorn that anyone could bring the prisoners a drink.

Among the multitude present and the countless others who clearly heard the announcement, not a single person came forward to offer so much as a drop of water.

By April of 1945 the Buchenwald train had been traveling for about two weeks, and it was impossible to tell how many people were still alive in the other cars. Early one morning the train began to move backward. It lurched along the track until it came to a standstill underneath an important bridge.

American planes not only dominated the skies, but there were so many in the air that they were turning day into night. This is why the train had stopped where it did. Prisoners who had been used as slaves, stonemasons, machinists, donkeys, rubble clearers, sanitation workers, and objects of torture were now being used as human shields.

The Germans correctly assumed that when the pilots would swoop down to bomb their target they would see hundreds of civilians in the open cars and hold their fire. This is in fact what happened, and when some of the pilots swung around a second time to observe the train close up, they fell victim to German antiaircraft fire.

After the bridge was saved, the train continued to roll away from the Allies, stopping from time to time so that the officers could cook themselves a meal. The starving prisoners were let loose in the fields to scavenge for something vaguely edible to put in their mouths. The desperate captives even sucked the earth to try to extract some moisture.

One time Salek noticed a rock glistening with dew in the early morning sun, so he licked the rock as if it were a lollipop. He was always on the lookout for nettles. He had eaten so many of them that he had become immune to their sting. Salek then repeated an earlier error when he found a sugar beet that the farmers had not considered worthy of gathering. It was caked in mud and decomposing, but at the time it was a delicious treat. Alas, the outcome of this feast was once again a dreadful bout of diarrhea.

Sitting beside Salek on a bench of corpses was a redhead who looked about twelve years old, but could easily have been five. He spoke a beautiful Lithuanian Yiddish and the two bemoaned their departure from Buchenwald. They had heard that the day after commencing their railway to hell, the camp had been liberated.

The agony of the two knew no bounds. They were unaware that the Americans arrived too late for most of the Jewish prisoners. The Germans had taken them out into the forests and shot them. Although the war was all but over and the Nazis were running for their lives, the war against the Jews continued, *über alles*.

Salek continued to talk to the redhead until he fell silent. Closer inspection revealed that he was dead; out like a light.

After so many days on the train one could only speculate where the next stop would be. The survivors all had different opinions, but Salek surmised that heading to a different labor camp was untenable, for by this point no one was fit for work. The remaining option was elimination.

Men in their late twenties (from Salek's point of view "the older generation") contemplated suicide. They had often seen the Russian POWs take their lives by either slitting their veins against the locks of the boxcars or by biting into their wrist arteries. Sometimes they would solicit the assistance of a friend to choke or suffocate; all were very violent deaths.

A man in his thirties solemnly declared, "We Jews do not commit suicide. We have been committed to death, but if we die, let us die *leshem Shomayim* and with *kavod* (for the sake of Heaven and with honor). Let us show them that we die as Jews and that we are not afraid of death. We will not surrender our belief in the World to Come."

The man's brief speech created a mood of sobriety, and the prisoners continued to wonder what would happen next. Normally, it is human nature to hope for the best and fantasize that a miracle may yet happen. For those entrapped within the Holocaust, "normal" was an abnormal concept.

Ironically, the thought of liberation never crossed their minds. They were obsessed with death. And as they contemplated what form their deaths would take, whether at their own hands or that of the enemy, a different reality set in. Independent of the older man's warning, suicide was not a simple procedure. They didn't have the tools to cut their throats or veins, and the way the Russians did it was very crude, cruel, and so...un-Jewish!

The next day the train stopped at a small station near a German village. The *transportfuhrer* ordered all of the Russian POWs to detrain at once, and three hundred to four hundred emaciated souls slowly disembarked from the train. The *transportfuhrer* looked them over and marched them away. After about half an hour the huddled mass was still visible in the distance, entering a small forest of white-barked trees, and then they were seen no more.

The death train remained at the same spot overnight. During the night, a fierce storm erupted. Through the blinding rain, howling wind, and terrifying lightning, the starving prisoners lifted their mouths heavenward to quench their parched lips.

At some point during that wretched night, Salek finally managed to close his eyes. He beheld a vision so vivid he could not tell if he was dreaming or not. He was visited by Rochel, the blue-eyed girl with whom he had fallen in love at Skarzysko. "I've found you," she whispered. "I told you I'd find you! And now we can go home. Your parents are here!"

Salek looked around and sure enough, he saw all of the members of his family. Rochel tried to reach out to touch him, and he tried to reach her – but neither succeeded.

Salek feared that it was just a dream. He wanted to touch something to make sure that he was not hallucinating. He confronted harsh reality in the morning when he awoke in the same filthy car.

Eventually the journey to hell recommenced. After about two hours the train came to a stop at a small red station that looked like a Swiss chalet, complete with geraniums in the window boxes. The *transportfuhrer*, accompanied by SS guards, growled, "Not all the Russians have left the train. This is your last chance to come down; otherwise we'll shoot you on the spot."

The remaining Russians were ordered to pick up shovels. Some of them did not understand the instructions and were shot for their failure to respond. The rest did as they were ordered and marched off. The Jewish veterans of Nazi policy sympathized with the Soviet POWs, understanding that they would be forced to dig their own graves. Their suspicions were confirmed several hours later when gunshots were heard.

The journey resumed and Salek was no longer afraid of death, just determined. Determined to leave this world as a Jew. After all, they were being murdered simply because they were Jews. Salek repeated to himself, "*Shema Yisrael Hashem Elokeinu Hashem Echad!*" He must have said it a hundred times so that when his time would come, he wouldn't hesitate or forget what to say; it would emerge spontaneously.

Throughout the four and a half weeks of the train ride to hell from Buchenwald, the only thought that occupied Salek's mind, other than death, was Rochel. This memory alone kept him going, and all he could envision and dream about was her.

More and more corpses were removed, and still, the *transportfuhrer* inspected each car to make sure that there were no Russians left. He looked for green fatigues or a military jacket, and when he found what he was looking for he did not waste any time, often shooting them on the spot. He obviously had orders to eliminate any Russian prisoners and he fulfilled his command with Prussian precision.

***

There are no words to describe the final days of the train trip. All of the pain and agony of the previous six years paled next to what Salek was experiencing. There were days on end without food or water. All the while, he also suffered from diarrhea. With no facilities to relieve himself, Salek had few options. He did not even attempt to lower his trousers, and remained standing at all times so that the wind would help dry his soiled rags. It was impossible to sit anyway, as his strained skin rubbed torturously against his bones.

The last two or three days the train stopped every few hours. Sometimes it stopped in a wooded area, enabling the inmates to stretch out their matchstick arms and snatch leaves off the trees. These leaves served as their solitary sustenance. By this stage there was room to maneuver in the train car; only a fraction of those who had departed from Buchenwald were still alive.

At the beginning of May the train arrived at a German town that was in ruins. Salek cheered at the destruction wrought upon Germany. From there they rumbled past several stations in the Sudeten region of Czechoslovakia. Following the Munich Conference, this district had been incorporated into Germany. Finally, in an open field, a dozen Czech freedom fighters with red armbands commandeered the train.

They forced open the door to the officers' car, but the villains had already escaped. Only a few Hungarian guards remained, and one of them displayed orders that the consignment of prisoners was to be delivered to Theresienstadt. It was May 9, 1945, a full day after the war was over – but they were the last to know.

Chapter Thirteen

A Flicker of Hope

Although the war was over; Salek's uphill battle for recovery was just beginning. He recounted:

I was far too weak to get down. Had I attempted to jump off the train, I would have broken countless bones. I was quite certain that I would be presumed dead and left on the train. I kept repeating, *'Shema Yisrael Hashem Elokeinu Hashem Echad.'* I could not resolve my dilemma: Should I say it now, or should I wait until later? What if I am no longer able to say it then, right before death?

The leader of the partisans instructed the engineer to drive the train to Theresienstadt. Within half a day we arrived at what looked like a concentration camp. The officers were removed from the train and marched off. They told us to remain on the train and we'd be taken care of by their medical personnel.

A couple of open trucks arrived carrying bread and other foodstuffs, but it was too great a strain for me to investigate further. They tried to distribute bread to the people on the wagon. It had been weeks since we had seen bread. Some of the stronger prisoners among us jumped down and attempted to run toward the bread, creating bedlam. This made the partisans really panic. Our behavior was far more akin to animals than human beings. They were also scared – understandably – by the sight of living skeletons clearly carrying contagious diseases running amok.

It took them several hours before they could distribute all the bread. I did not get any because I could hardly move. Instead of cutting slices they threw whole loaves, which was a big mistake. We were unable to bite into the loaves as our lips were dry and our gums were sore. The solitary piece in my range was a chunk that someone else had gotten hold of and had accidentally dropped on the floor of the wagon. However, I couldn't even use my hand to pick it up and bring it to my mouth, let alone consume it. I was just too weak to do anything, even to save my life.

Night fell and the train moved very, very slowly into the camp. About twenty men and women wearing white coats gathered around the train. They lifted people off and wheeled them away into Theresienstadt on trolleys which they had prepared by the side of the track. They unloaded the Russian POWs as well, and despite the *transportfuhrer*'s best efforts, there was one compartment full of them at the rear, next to the *Totenwagen*. I heard that they were the only ones who had engaged in cannibalism, consuming portions from the corpses. Of the six or seven thousand people who left Buchenwald with me, very few remained.

They lifted me off the wagon, but they could not put me down anywhere because I had no flesh. Assisting in this procedure were German girls about sixteen and seventeen years old, dressed in blue overalls. These were the very girls who had danced and slept with the German officers. They had been dragged out of their villages and arrested by the Czech freedom fighters who brought them to Theresienstadt to help look after the survivors. Each of these girls was wearing a white headscarf. The Czechs had shaved their heads as a mark of shame and to prevent them from slipping away in civilian disguise.

I was placed into a blanket and gently carried inside the camp. As they washed me down, I overheard one telling the other that I would have to be sent to "Nazareth," which turned out to be the infirmary. Four bald German girls each held a corner of the blanket to transport me to "Nazareth." They located some string and jerry-rigged my blanket into an improvised hammock. Suspended from the ceiling in a soft cocoon, all I wanted was to be left alone so that I could settle my emotions. I wasn't hungry, I wasn't thirsty, I wasn't sleepy; I was in a state that medical science may not have a term for.

My only faculty that was operating properly was my eyesight, and I gazed up at the ceiling all the time. In the state that I was in, nothing had any meaning for me. Not survival, not the end of the war, not the beginning of the war, not my parents, not my family, not what I was going to do next. Nothing.

Theresienstadt was filled with personalities and professionals: doctors, professors, musicians, poets – the elite of the Jewish nation evicted from their homes in Prague and Berlin. One of Theresienstadt's doctors shouted to one of the girls to lower the hammock and support my head. Using a wooden spoon, she poured some liquid into my mouth. My lips were so fragile that had she used a metal spoon she might have easily cut me. The spoon felt big and bulky against my lips but the liquid flowing into my mouth reaffirmed my humanity.

A day or so later, I was lowered and taken to another ward with a white ceiling. I was told that I had a Red Cross package waiting for me. I certainly had no strength to open it. It was then that I was fed my first piece of bread. I couldn't swallow it so I just chewed and chewed. I couldn't taste the bread at all, but at least I felt its texture. They removed my clothing and washed my body down with lukewarm water.

This was my first encounter in years with human kindness. I was in such a daze that I didn't know what to make of what was transpiring. My mind was not functioning properly and I was having trouble grasping if I was fully liberated or if the war was still raging but this area was liberated. Once I started to recover, questions tumbled out at a frantic pace: Where am I to go now? Back to Buchenwald? Back to Skarzysko? Back to Transilow? Back to Apt, my hometown? What would happen? I had no family, no home, no country, no language, no education, no job, no future at all. I still was unable to read or talk or do anything at all. I just lay motionless with questions raging through my head.

In the next room, there were former prisoners like myself, but older – in their twenties or even thirties – shouting, crying, and screaming. The nurses said that some of them were mad. Some were calling out the names of their dear ones – wives, sons, daughters. "Moishela, Chanala, where are you?" they demanded. It was heart-rending. I thought my experiences had hardened me, yet I was unprepared for such raw emotions; it was simply unbearable. In a way it was even worse than the transports or Buchenwald. There, people would die quietly without commotion. They would just close their eyes, perhaps utter a final sigh, and then we knew that they had taken their last breath.

In the morning, I noticed that my clothing, the "uniform" that I had inherited from Buchenwald, had been taken away from me. It had been full of lice and vermin. My skin looked like a sieve; I was constantly covered in dots of blood. I then remembered that when my redhaired friend died, I went through his pockets before he was removed to the *toteswagen* with the other corpses. In his pocket he had a page torn from a siddur and a couple of German coins. His father had told him, "Don't forget to say '*Shema Yisrael*' every day." He had kept the page in his pocket and said the first *parasha* of *Shema* every day.

I asked the doctor about it and she answered, "I'm afraid your clothing was burned."

The young Jewish doctor came back and spoke to me from time to time. She spoke many languages and was obviously well educated and highly intelligent. She informed me that the Red Cross had arranged for survivors to be sent to Switzerland, but her words did not register.

In the midst of all my misery my hearing came back, and that was a harbinger for future progress. After about ten days, I stood up on my own feet for the first time, although I still couldn't walk. Two girls supported me and I limped into a big hall filled with chairs. It looked like a theater. On the stage was a collection of musical instruments.

I noticed a violin and asked if I could touch it. I picked it up and played a note and it was apparent to those present that I knew how to handle a bow. "'A' sounds correct," I commented, "It is tuned properly." The attendant told me that if I'd be here long enough, I could join the concert musicians. She mentioned composers who had survived, who wrote music here or had brought music and instruments with them. She also offered to bring me back to listen to a performance. This never happened because I was transferred to another section in Theresienstadt for people who had slightly recovered.

Gradually, I was able to walk unaided. After a couple of weeks, a milestone occurred when I lined up for the first time for my coffee and bread by myself. It was a novelty to hold a slice of bread in my hand and enjoy the chewing. It had been years since I'd eaten a piece of bread non-clandestinely and without fear. Out of habit, I broke off half the slice and put it in my pocket.

A nurse came along and told me that they'd received a consignment from the Red Cross and there was a package for every prisoner. My package was about one to one and a half square feet and quite heavy. I tried to open it, but it was beyond my ability.

This was actually for the best; had I consumed the food they had sent, it would have been too much for my stomach to manage and might have proven fatal.

When I felt strong enough I was free to walk out of the camp to the nearby town called Leitmeritz. Many of the former prisoners had already been to Leitmeritz and helped themselves to anything of value in abandoned German homes. I was terribly jealous of all the watches, clocks, and other objects that they had taken.

As soon as I recovered, a rapid process, thank God, I made my way to town, first displaying my pass to the Russian guard at the gate. I did not actually possess a pass, but someone told me, "Don't be silly, take a scrap of printed paper, flatten it down to make it look nice and show it to the illiterate guard." I found a little printed advertisement and waved it in front of him.

In town I saw a German officer, a tall, broad man. He was leading a horse and wagon and looked a shabby sight without any weapons and the badge ripped off his military cap. The only decent thing he still possessed was a pair of beautiful leather boots.

Boldly, I shouted out "Halt!" in his direction. He could see that I was not a German, nor a local citizen, but one of the survivors. "What have you got hidden there inside your boots? Take them off and show me."

He answered "*Garnichts! Ich habe Garnichts versteckt.* Nothing, I have nothing hidden." I was having none of it. "*Ausziehen*! Take them off!" I ordered. He sat down at the roadside, took them off and handed them to me. Of course there was nothing at all concealed inside them. Once I had the boots and after making him empty out all of his pockets, I ordered him to stand up and march away, and that is just what he did. There was definitely a sense of satisfaction in seeing a high-ranking German officer marching off in his socks! However, a Russian officer passing by looked at the boots admiringly and asked if he could try them on. His own boots were worn right through and the soles were nonexistent.

According to his tale, he had walked in his boots all the way from Stalingrad! He liked this pair at once and they were a good fit. He gave me his old boots and walked off. I took his pair, which stank terribly, and threw them over the bridge and into the river.

All I was left with was the contents of the German officer's pockets: a lighter, a pipe, some tobacco, other bits and pieces, and a large bundle of deutschmarks. I had been told that since the Germans had lost the war, their currency had no value, and I threw the whole lot into the river. But I was sadly misinformed. The money was still worth every penny of its former value! I returned to the camp no wealthier than when I had left, but with lightness in my heart. Standing up to the German officer was another step forward in my recovery.

Chapter Fourteen

The Beginning of a Long Recuperation

That same week, the doctor informed me that I would be X-rayed to determine if I had tuberculosis. I would then be sent somewhere to recover, but certain nations would not accept tubercular victims. He mentioned various countries, including Switzerland, England, France, and Holland, but to me they were all the same. I didn't have relatives in any of those places, nor did I speak their languages.

Tests revealed that I had tuberculosis. Thus, England and a few other countries were out of the question. I was in Theresienstadt for another two weeks when a man I'd never met informed me that I'd be going to Prague.

I was transported to Prague on a Russian horse and wagon and accommodated in a former school building. I was given a physical examination and informed that the Red Cross had set up a tracing service where I could register my name and inquire after family members. Every time a new batch of survivors arrived in Prague, the streets would fill with Jews straining to recognize someone.

I paid a visit to the Red Cross and made friends with the leader of the Jewish Brigade, who ran the family tracing bureau. I explained that I thought I had family in Palestine and asked if he could help me get there. He detailed the route as if it were as easy as switching stations on the London Underground.

"Take a train from Prague to Pilsen, then from Pilsen to Austria, and then from Austria to Italy. In Bari, we will take you to Palestine through the *Aliyah Bet.*"

I knew that arrangements were being made for tubercular people like myself, but I still wished to keep my options open. Not having lost any of my gumption, I approached the British Embassy and requested to see the consul, explaining that I was a British citizen wishing to return to Palestine. They allowed me into a large waiting room that was clean and well furnished. They then brought me a cup of tea with milk, something that I had never had in my life. It could very well be that as all these pleasantries were taking place I was actually being observed by officials from another room.

Eventually, an elderly gentleman emerged to speak with me. I related to him that I was born in Haifa and had come to Poland prior to the war. I was captured by the Germans and incarcerated in a concentration camp. He asked if I had any identification. I replied that my sole identification was my number from Buchenwald and then realized that I'd made a mistake. If they bothered to check the Buchenwald records, my fib was over.

More tea was served, along with cakes, bread, and margarine. The wizened consul told me that although they couldn't issue a visa on the spot, they would write a letter attesting that I was "presumed" British. The letter would be useful with the Czech officials.

Thanks to this document I secured a temporary visa to remain in Czechoslovakia for six months. I still have most of these papers and they are the only official record of who I am and where I came from – as bogus as the information is. Based on them I receive my pension.

I was also issued two books of ration stamps and a small allowance of money. In my own mind, I was all set for Palestine via *Aliyah Bet.*

When I got back to my lodgings, I was informed that within a day or two we would all be flown to England. This was anything but good news to me. I had absolutely no interest in living in England. I had no family or friends there. Switzerland, France, and Holland appealed to me much more. In the *lager* I had met many people from all these European countries, but I had never met a Briton, and the people, language, and culture seemed too foreign to be worthy of consideration. I bemoaned the situation with a group of twenty or so friends, none of whom were pleased with the idea of going to England. Since we were unanimous in our decision, we decided to take a train to Pilsen, which was in the American zone. We could then make our way to Bari and ultimately to Palestine.

At the border, for the first time, I encountered American soldiers wearing their odd-looking helmets. No matter how much we begged and pleaded, insisting that we were survivors from Auschwitz and Buchenwald, the Americans would not let us through. They had no linguistic ability at all and did not understand a word that was not in Yankee-Doodle English.

It was getting late and they didn't know what to do with us, so they put us in a compound and locked us in. It was so cold there that I thought I would die from exposure. Some cold, flavorless coffee was brought to us.

Early in the morning we were sent back to Prague, dejected and defeated. The doctor in charge of us was furious with us. Where had we been? They had been searching the streets for us all night. They thought that perhaps we had been kidnapped or had maybe even committed suicide.

We told him our story, and he said we were crazy for playing such a dangerous game. Furthermore, that afternoon we were to have been X-rayed before flying to England; otherwise they would not let us in. It was too late for that now, so he simply took out the form, stamped it, and signed that we were in the clear. I don't believe my tuberculosis would have been an issue for him, X-ray or not.

Several buses appeared to take all 270 of us to an airfield outside Prague. We flew via Holland in a dozen Lancaster bombers. We landed at Keswick, in Cumbria, and settled into a hostel run by the Central British Fund.

This was the first time that as a group we met Jewish representatives of organizations in Palestine: *Hashomer Hatzair, Agudat Yisrael,* and several others.

Rabbi Yitzchok Tuvia Weiss, *ztz"l,* a wonderful educator, sportsman, and human being, led and guided us. Although not everyone in the group had come from a religious family, he saw to it that we were all provided with a proper Jewish education and a familiarity with English life. Rabbi Weiss and his team also endeavored to instill within us a modicum of civilization and decorum. We were far removed from manners and hygiene and had to be taught how to eat, wash, brush our teeth, and how to perform various acts of daily living. I hadn't brushed my teeth or changed my clothing in nearly five years!

Eventually we were divided; we couldn't all attend the same school. I was sent to a boarding school in London with about fifty other refugees. We tried our best to conform to the regulations. The teaching staff was mostly of German origin, so they taught us English with a German accent!

When Leonard Montefiore, who was on the teaching staff, saw my notebooks he exclaimed, "Salek Orenstein, you don't belong here. I'll make arrangements for you to go to a private school. It's expensive, and you must work very hard to make our investment in you worthwhile, but I'm sure the right thing for you is to see Miss Nixon at Cricklewood." I was still unused to people caring about me so much. I was very lucky that so many people really wanted to help make a difference in my life and those of so many other survivors.

Chapter Fifteen

It Was Love at First Sight (Yes, First Sight!)

I never thought that I would settle down in England. But thank God things were blessed from the outset. I met many good people, who became good friends, and their help and influence made a big difference. Two years after my arrival in England, I reunited with my sister Pola. She had survived the war in Russia and was married to Tulek, a Jew who had served in the Polish resistance against the Nazi occupation of Poland. Pola and Tulek had made their life in Kiryat Chaim in Israel, and had a daughter who was named after our mother. In the most miraculous of ways, God enabled me to survive and continue in the footsteps of my forefathers. I was grateful to be involved in creating a new Jewish nation out of the remnants of the inferno that was the Holocaust.

The very greatest gift of all is my dear wife. I was thunderstruck the moment I met her. It happened at Hasmonean School in London, while attending my friend's wedding. During the *chuppa*

I noticed the most beautiful young lady I had ever seen. She wore a royal blue dress with a pink sash around her waist and carried a little white handbag. All I wanted was to get nearer to her and exchange a few words.

Gingerly I approached Jenny Merel, and although I do not have a history of being timid, I was as bashful as could be. The closer I got the more beauty, refinement, and femininity I saw. I held my breath when I introduced myself and resumed breathing when she courteously returned my greetings. I asked her if she would date me. She told me that this was not possible; she was going away to Switzerland with her family. "Would you send me a card?" I pleaded. I wished there to be some connection between us. Standing at the drinks table, I was struck by the irony that I had attended the wedding in order to toast a *lechayim* for my friend, but in fact I was drinking a *lechayim* for myself.

Postscript

This narration is a tiny window through which may be glimpsed only part of the whole onslaught of suffering endured by my people. I only wish more people would relate their stories, as I have done here.

I pray to the Creator to give voice to those whose innocent blood was spilled and those reduced to ashes in the crematoria. May He haunt the cruel murderers and their generations after them, who perpetrated such unimaginable atrocities only for our crime of being Jewish. May the so-called leaders of the non-Jewish world of that time also be called upon in judgment for their silence and indifference to the fate of the Jews.

Salek Orenstein

Afterword

I telephoned her many times, but I was unsuccessful in making a date. I was so delighted when she posted a card. Eventually I prevailed and we went out to a concert at the Old Vic near Waterloo, and after that to a music hall in Kingsway. As hard as it was to summon the courage in my initial approach, an equal amount was necessary to propose to her outside her brother's house at 23 Downage in Hendon, London. The fact that I was not rejected immediately was a relief beyond description. She replied that she would first have to discuss it with her brother, and a few days later we were engaged!

I remember that when I brought my *kalla* a bouquet of flowers, she was wearing a white blouse tied with a ribbon, and I felt that I had never seen a more beautiful sight in my entire life. When she smiled, her delicately sculpted cheeks were full of sweetness. This memory will never leave me, and I see my darling wife in the same light now as I did the very first day I saw her.

Baruch Hashem, we were married on September 7, 1954, and my happiness then was greater than I could ever have imagined.

As I stood beneath the *chuppa,* my heart was filled with immense gratitude to Hashem, who saw fit to keep me alive. I thought of my parents, and believed that only their heavenly intervention could have brought about this wonderful moment. In Jenny, I found again the father, the mother, the brother, and the little sister whom I had lost in the Holocaust. She was the embodiment of all that I could dream and wish for.

Our son was born in July 1955. He was a most beautiful little boy, exactly the image of my wife. We named him Hershy, after my father. When I held my child, I could not find the words to express my thankfulness to Hashem. Wheeling his carriage around the block of Vincent Court, where we started our married life, filled me with indescribable pride. Two years later, our darling daughter was born and we named her Mindy after Jenny's mother.

After Mindy's birth, the well-known Rabbi, Reb Elchanan Halpern, came to see me, collecting for his yeshiva. "Salek Orenstein," he said, "now you have fulfilled the mitzva of *peru urevu.* You have two children, one of each, a girl and a boy."

We moved from our warm group of friends at Vincent Court to a house at 51 Rowsley Avenue in Hendon. The house was modest and in disrepair. My wife had lost her parents and I had lost mine, but now we had each other and a little family of our own.

The next arrival was a lovely little boy, born on Purim, with a smile on his face! We named him Shmuli after Jenny's father. I shall never forget how at home before he was born, my wife was standing and preparing plentiful *mishloach manos* as per her generous nature. She must have prepared about thirty little baskets, and as she was carefully tying up the ribbons, she murmured, "Darling, I'm afraid I have to go the hospital – the pains are coming every minute now."

I rushed to get the car ready, and then we drove off to Bearsted Hospital. Jenny was admitted to the ward, and in no time, I saw a nurse wheeling a little trolley with a bundle on top of it in my direction. "*Mazal tov*!" the nurse wished me. I dashed to the room where my wife was and saw her smiling face as she sat up in bed sipping a cup of tea.

After Shmuli was born, we sought to enlarge our wonderful family even more. Four years later, on Hoshana Rabba, our fourth child was born. We named him Avraham Yosef (Josy) after one of our ancestors who was a great *talmid chacham*. The joy, happiness, satisfaction, and contentment were so great that I lack the ability to describe the emotions.

I had established my own business, and with the help of God, it was successful. I always attributed my good fortune to the fact that I had my darling Jenny by my side. She was the fount of my success.

Only in one aspect was my happiness not complete. I always felt that having been blessed with survival, my place was in Israel with *Am Yisrael*. I was always conscious of my duty to be part and parcel of the rebirth of the Jewish nation, and in my heart I felt it was there where I really belonged.

In 1983, our beloved daughter Mindy and our dear son-in-law Johnny Ebrahimoff informed us that they had decided to make aliya. In no time we decided to buy an apartment in Jerusalem. In my life I have been faced with numerous occasions upon which I was forced to make critical decisions in an instant. When I saw the apartment at 5 Rechov Diskin, Kiryat Wolfson, my decision was instantaneous. We signed the papers the next day.

Our love for the city grew with each visit. Every time we left, I was filled with a certain nostalgia and sorrow. I knew that this was where I belonged and where I always should have been from the moment of my liberation. Our daughter, son-in-law, and grandchildren, Cobi, Benjy, and D'vora, reside in Petach Tikva where Mindy has a successful career as a midwife. I am so proud of her profession. After the systematic destruction of our people that I witnessed, I see that my own daughter – the odds of her own birth defying the statistics – spends her life bringing new Jewish babies into the world. I am so happy. My heart is full.

Eulogy for My Father

2 Kislev 5764 (November 27, 2003), Har Hamenuchot Cemetery, Jerusalem

My father, Salek *z"l*, died at age seventy-five after bravely battling illness with incredible strength and with every fiber of his being for the entire five years that he suffered. It was suffering of the highest order, yet he fought on. He fought daily, and he fought throughout the nights. He fought in hospitals and he fought at home. He fought long and hard, just as stubbornly as when he was a young boy in Nazi labor camps. He fought with the same resilience, perseverance, and strength, but with one difference – he was not alone; my mother תבדל"א – never left his side. Throughout my father's illness, she was his guardian angel. For him, knowing that this angel was constantly there, made his life a little easier.

***

One of the most difficult predicaments I know of, aside from cracking a secret code, is for a survivor of Nazi atrocities in the 1940s to describe his experience to someone who was not in Europe during that time – in a manner that will ensure the listener's full understanding and empathy.

Throughout my early childhood and adolescence, it seemed as though my father's tales of the Holocaust were contained in a code that was undecipherable to most of the people I observed who listened as he told them. I could see their faces; I heard their incredulous responses. Only other survivors knew the code, I sensed.

Daddy, perhaps your stories were understood to a certain extent, but far short of the implications of their malevolent, excruciating reality, which even I as your child, the child of two survivors, could not presume to imagine.

What you told me about the years before and during the war, I pictured with great confusion, anxiety, and a kind of self-nurturing, insulating mental numbness. The truth is that the actual concept of the Holocaust was too much for me.

I suppose other people listened in a similar fashion, unable to absorb the urgency of such horror. I would remember the stories and spend many long nights wondering about your experiences in the dark before dawn.

A few years ago, after visiting your hometown Opatow in Poland, my nocturnal fears began to lie dormant. I visited your home; I saw the location where your *shtiebel* and *cheder* once stood – it was like opening an old album of family photographs. I suddenly felt an intimate strong sense of belonging and then I realized that the most important conclusion here is about the fortitude and endurance of your mind and heart at the center of all this horror and tragedy and your ability to retain a spiritual, religious, Jewish life with tenderness, compassion, and dignity, and illustrate the pure delight of being alive in the face of them.

Daddy, with this understanding, I am so proud of you. I now know that it is not an understanding reached because of the terrible events, but of the impact of what it means to be a human being and a Jew at the first indications of those events. It is through your simple and often touching recollections of life in Poland during the worst nightmare of the twentieth century, that a sense of that nightmare closer to the truth may be achieved.

If you have your way Daddy, we may now be a little closer to cracking the code.

Daddy, grief is the price we have to pay for love. You and I can't avoid the pain of parting, but Daddy, you've always taught me that we have to try and accept our lot lovingly. You told me that you had faced death so many times that you know the contours of his face and do not fear him; and now I know why.

When the body is sick, the spirit assists and supports the body with its sympathy and provides consolation, acceptance, and endurance. Your unquenchable human Jewish spirit which the Nazis tried to crush, but failed, is now not a part of history, but lives on.

We, your children, will continue with your hope, your courage, and your faith, because through your great love of us and Torah, we understand Hashem's love for our family.

You know what it means to sacrifice something for someone else and with this lesson, you have taught us by example how to shape our lives by Jewish values.

Daddy, you told me that you cried *Shema Yisrael* so many times during those years of hell because each day you feared was your last. One third of the Jewish population was wiped out – over six million victims.

Your life is the story of one who survived and I promise you Daddy, that we your children and grandchildren will do our utmost that your great love and respect for Yiddishkeit will live on through us, in a manner that will always make you proud.

How can we not?

In 1996 you presented me with a book compiled by Martin Gilbert called *The Boys*. It is the story of 732 young concentration camp survivors, children who shared wartime experiences that were terrible beyond imagination. Some of your personal experiences are recorded in that book. You dedicated that book to us as follows:

> To my dear children,
>
> May these horrific personal memories and testimonies of the very few Jewish survivors be an eternal documented lesson to all the future generations – to stand on guard against the antisemitic world who never relinquished its aim and wish to destroy us.
>
> Love, Dad, Saba, 4th November 1996

You, Daddy, bear witness to the strengths of the human spirit.

Today your *neshama* will be welcomed at the Gates of Gan Eden… as you approach the *Kiseh Hakavod,* I beg Hashem to recognize the great *emuna* you portrayed to defend His name.

Daddy, you were liberated once from Theriesenstadt and rebuilt your life in Britain and Israel. You showed great physical, mental, and emotional strength in establishing, together with Mummy, a beautiful Torah rich home and brought us up in it.

Today, you are liberated for the second and final time in your life. Go in peace, in dignity, and in freedom, wearing a tallit as is befitting for the devout Jew that you fought to be all your life.

We love you, but cannot keep you. You are not ours to keep.

Mindy

▲
Salek Orenstein at his grandson's bar mitzva, August 1993

Members of the Orensztajn family on holiday in Sandomierz before the war. Salek pictured bottom row on the left

Boys liberated by Czech partisans. Their train had been traveling from Buchenwald for a month. It was liberated at Theresienstadt on the day the war ended.

"The Boys" in Prague in front of the monument Jan Hus, on the day of their departure to England, August 1945

Salek Orenstein and Jenny Merel's wedding, September 7, 1954, London

Glossary

The following glossary provides a partial explanation of some of the foreign words and phrases used in this book. The spelling, tense, and explanations reflect the way the specific word is used in *Beyond Belief*. Often, there are alternate spellings and meanings for the words. Foreign words and phrases which are immediately followed by a translation in the text are not included in this section.

a nechtiger tug – (Yiddish, colloquial) impossible
Alef-Beis – the Hebrew alphabet
aliya – going up; term used in connection with being called up to the reading of the Torah or immigration to Israel
Aliyah Bet – illegal immigration to Israel during the British mandatory rule of Palestine
Am Yisrael – the Jewish nation
arbes – chickpeas
aron kodesh – literally, holy ark; ark containing the Torah scrolls
Baruch Hashem – literally, the Lord is blessed; thank God
beis hakevaros – cemetery

beis midrash – house of study used for both Torah study and prayer

bekisheh – (Yiddish) a long frock coat worn by men, often reserved for festive occasions

chas vechalila – God forbid

chazan – cantor; the leader of public worship

cheder – elementary school for religious studies

chevra kaddisha – literally, holy society; a group which provides for the religious needs of the community, regarding the care and rites of the dead

cholent – hot stew served on Shabbos

Chumash – the Five Books of Moses

chuppa – literally, wedding canopy; wedding ceremony

emuna – faith

Gemara – commentary on the Mishnah (together they comprise the Talmud); a volume of the Talmud

Gan Eden – literally, the Garden of Eden; paradise

gartel – (Yiddish) belt worn by some men, particularly Hasidim, during prayer

gleizalle tei – (Yiddish) a cup of tea

hakafos – joyous rotations with a Torah scroll

hamalach hagoel – prayer that the baby should receive heavenly protection

hamantaschen – triangular, jam- or poppyseed-filled cookies traditionally baked in honor of the Purim holiday

Hashem – literally, the Name; respectful reference to God

Hoshana Rabba – the seventh day of Sukkos

Hasid(im) – follower(s) of the teaching of the Baal Shem Tov

kalla – bride

kapo (German) – head of a unit

kapoteh – elegant caftan

kasher – to render kosher

kashrus – conforming to Jewish dietary regulations

Kiddush – sanctification; prayer recited over wine to usher in Shabbos and festivals
klezmer – (Yiddish) musicians; traditional Eastern European Jewish music
lechayim – to life (a toast)
lager – (German) camp
melamed – teacher
mi sheberach – prayer for an ill person's recovery
mikve – a ritual bath used for the purpose of ritual purification
mishloach manos – Purim delicacies sent to friends and neighbors
mitzva – literally, commandment; applied to good deeds
peru urevu – the commandment to be fruitful and multiply
paroches – curtain of the ark containing the Torah scrolls
parasha – chapter
psak – halachic decision
Purim – joyous religious festival commemorating the Jews' salvation from genocide
rabbanim - rabbis
Rashi – leading commentator on the Bible and Talmud
rav – rabbi
Reb Yid – polite form to address a fellow Jew
rebbe – (Yiddish) – rabbi, usually a Talmud teacher; instructor; hasidic leader
rebbetzin – rabbi's wife
refua shelema – have a complete recovery; customarily said to an ill person
sefer Torah – Torah scroll
seuda – festive meal
Shabbos – the Sabbath
shammes – synagogue attendant
Shema Yisrael Hashem Elokeinu Hashem Echad – prayer recited daily proclaiming the oneness of God and affirming faith in Him

shmatteh – (Yiddish) rag
shochet – (Hebrew) a ritual slaughterer
shtiebel(ach) – (Yiddish) small, informal intimate room for prayer or study
shtetl(ach) – (Yiddish) small village(s)
shtreimel(ach) – (Yiddish) decorative fur-trimmed hat worn by male hasidim on Sabbath and Festivals
shul – (Yiddish) synagogue
siddur – prayer book
simcha – literally, joy; celebration
tallis – four-cornered prayer shawl with fringes at each corner, worn by men during morning prayers
talmid chacham – Torah scholar
tefillin – black leather boxes containing numerous verses from the Bible bound to the arm and front of a man's head during morning prayers
Tehillim – Psalms
totenwagen – death cart
vayehi binsoa ha'aron – prayer when the Torah scroll is removed from its ark
vertel – (Yiddish) a short Torah thought
yahrzeit – (Yiddish) anniversary of a death
yeshiva ketana – religious school for teenage boys
yingel – (Yiddish) little boy
zeide – (Yiddish) grandfather
z"l – abbreviation for "May the memory of this righteous person be for a blessing"